Everything Democrats Hoped You'd Forget

by Michael O'Rourke

Copyright © 2024 by Michael O'Rourke

All rights reserved. No part of this book may be used or reproduced in any manner whatsoever without prior written consent of the author, except as provided by the United States of America copyright law.

Published by Tolle Lege Press, a division of Bravera Holdings, LLC.
3330 Cobb Pkwy. Ste. 324-346
Acworth, GA 30101
TolleLegePress.com

ISBN: 979-8-9857901-8-4

Editing by Liz Martin

This book is dedicated to my mom (whom I love and miss dearly) and to my Dad who sacrificed greatly on behalf of America and who once told me, "We cannot let this country fall into the wrong hands!"

This content in this publication is designed to employ humor, irony, and exaggeration to comment on societal issues, in a lighthearted and comedic manner, with the intention of provoking thought or amusement. The content presented in this publication is satirical.

Quoted statements and/or sources have not been footnoted or sourced. It is up to the sole discretion of the reader to locate and examine sourced/quoted material found in the content of this publication.

This publication is produced with the understanding that neither the author or the publisher is engaged or attempting to engage in rendering any legal, political, economic, scientific, or any other professional services.

Errors, misspellings, typos, improper punctuation, grammar, or syntax, or omissions are inherent risks in any publishing endeavor, and acknowledging the potential for mistakes, oversights, or negligence that may occur despite our best efforts, we thank the reader for their understanding.

The Author and the Publisher and their officers, directors, employees, family, friends, and agents are indemnified and held harmless from and against any and all claims, damages, losses, liabilities, costs, and expenses (including attorneys' fees) arising out of or related to any omission or inclusion of material within this publication.

Introduction

Welcome to a journey through the annals of recent history unlike any other.

In this unique collection, we invite you to explore pivotal moments, forgotten failures, figures that seem more at home in a fiction novel than reveled over in mainstream media, and forgotten tales of incredible incompetence, all brought to you through a lens of satire and humor.

Drawing from a myriad of sources and perspectives, O'Rourke presents a fresh and entertaining take on recent headlines regarding failures, fiascos, and fumbling faux pas created by members of the Democratic Party. His narrative is infused with wit, whimsy, and irreverence, and calls you not to forget the travesties assuaged upon the American people at the hands of the party least interested in serving the American people.

Prepare to embark on a delightful romp through recent events, where the serious and solemn are juxtaposed against incredulity and levity. As we navigate the corridors of recent history, O'Rourke invites you to suspend disbelief, and to revel in the absurdity of Democratic folly — all with a stern warning that history must not be allowed to repeat itself.

So join me as we journey through the last few years, guided by the twin beacons of satire and levity, to rediscover the moments that shaped our world for the worse under the regimes of Democrats in the Oval Office.

In this lighthearted exploration of history, we find not only a form of entertainment but also a deeper understanding of the human condition and the timeless truths that transcend the ages: the only hope for our children and their children and this great country we call our home is to elect America First candidates.

–Liz Martin
Co-author of The 1896 Prophecies

JANUARY

1. (2020) "It's time for the millionaires to pay their fair share!" Elizabeth Warren, who endlessly attacks the greed and self-interest of America's "millionaires and billionaires who wage war on America's middle class," proves once again she is arguably Washington's ultimate hypocrite when records reveal she earned more than $1.6 million but gave a paltry 2.7 percent to charity.

2. (2023) After putting in a Freedom of Information Act (FOIA) request to obtain training materials from various government agencies related to the Biden Administration's Diversity, Equity, and Inclusion program, the Wall Street Journal published an editorial entitled, "The U.S. Government's Woke Training."

Among other absurdities, the report reveals The Department of Veterans Affairs now has a "Gender Gingerbread Person" presumably to satisfy the pronoun police by killing off the suddenly offensive (but long beloved) "Gingerbread Man!" Additionally, if U.S. Army servicewomen express "discomfort showering with a female who has male genitalia," the brass orders them to "toughen up!"

The piece continues on to point out that commanders have the discretion to take reasonable measures to enhance privacy for all concerned. They can put up shower curtains, dividers, and the like. But, most importantly, they can't do so in a way that "ostracizes transgender personnel." It further reads, "It is Defense Department policy that service members will be treated according to the gender identity they have officially registered with!"

3. (2017) After Valerie Jarrett, President Obama's chief adviser and family friend, proudly announces that Barack's administration was "scandal free" during his eight years in office, Breitbart News, presents this (abbreviated) list of 18 of the admin's scandals, including Benghazi, the IRS' selective targeting of Conservative groups including the Tea Party and Fox News, Hillary Clinton's server, the NSA spying scandal, Solyndra, the Iran nuclear deal and "ransom" payment in which Barack Obama encouraged Iran to pursue nuclear power by paying billions of taxpayer dollars to use at their discretion, spying on AP journalists and James Rosen of Fox News, the Bowe Bergdahl prisoner swap in which deserter Bergdahl left his post to fraternize with the Taliban while US soldiers died searching for him (Obama

ultimately traded him for 5 high profile, violent, pro Taliban prisoners) the VA death list scandal in which the Department of Veterans Affairs put veterans on secret death lists while executives turned in phony status reports and signed themselves up for big bonuses and, last but not least, the Steele dossier and Hillary's criminal complicity in creating the fabricated "Russia-Collusion Hoax," in an attempt to take down duly-elected President Trump. Aside from this (partial) list a case could be made that Obama's 8-year reign was "scandal-free."

4. (2022) An animated (almost life-like) Joe Biden makes a passionate speech in which he vows to defend the nation's founding ideals from the threats posed by the violent mob that stormed the Capitol one year earlier. Biden harkens back to critical moments from the nation's past, casting the "insurrection" as a living symbol of the inflection point in American history. He makes no mention of the "inflection point" that occurred the day of his Inauguration, which marked the first time a president who was compromised by decades of business dealings with the Chinese Communist Party began residing in the White House.

5. (2020) A CNN spokesperson confirms the news outlet has settled a lawsuit with Kentucky high school student, Nicholas Sandmann, a pro-life student who was at the center of a viral video controversy in which he was mocked and maligned by the network. The local outlet said a settlement figure was not made public at a court hearing in Covington, Kentucky. Apparently, the network was unable to use "Hey, everybody knows we're fake news" as a defense.

6. (2021) "I hurt for our country. All I know is that now is a time for true patriotism. Now is the time for those who voted for this president to see the reality of what they've supported and publicly and forcefully rebuke him and the actions of that mob." Michelle Obama sounds off blaming President Trump for the January 6 protests in DC. She continues citing her "unwavering love of our country!" Amazingly she is able to keep a straight face while making the remark.

7. (2021) "No one can tell me that if it had been a group of BLM protesting yesterday, they wouldn't have been treated very, very differently from the mob of thugs that stormed the Capitol. We all know that's true, and it's unacceptable. Totally unacceptable." Joe Biden fumes after he (supposedly) receives a text message from his 21-year-old granddaughter, Finnegan

Biden, claiming the police were ultra-aggressive with BLM as compared to the way Jan 6 protestors were treated.

The dozens of Jan 6 protestors being held in a DC jail in such squalid that they have requested to be moved to GITMO might beg to differ. The political prisoners cite "black mold, worms on the walls and in their food, abuse by guards and vaccine requirements among the hardships they face. They also report their clothing returns from the laundry "covered in brown stains, pubic hair and reeking of ripe urine." Additionally, the say they have lost their eyesight and hair because of "malnourishment." Meanwhile, violent BLM protestors and ANTIFA are living large. Finnegan's comments stand as proof that the leftist miscreant doesn't fall far from the tree.

8. (2022) Nancy Pelosi scrambles to quash bipartisan efforts to ban stock trading by Congressional lawmakers - even as she and her husband have raked in as much as $30 million from bets on the Big Tech firms Pelosi is responsible for regulating. Late last month, the House Speaker disclosed that the Pelosis scooped up millions of dollars in "bullish call options, including Google, Salesforce, Micron Technology and Roblox" at the same time some insiders say she stalled efforts to rein in Big tech."

Days later, Pelosi brushed off worries over stock picking by lawmakers claiming it was part of "the free-market economy," comments that reportedly made Dem insiders "blood boil," according to people close to the speaker. Jeff Hauser, a self-proclaimed progressive Democrat and founder and director of the Revolving Door Project, tells The Post stock picking by elected officials "gets worrisome about whether legislators have access to insider information or whether your stock purchases will consciously or unconsciously impact policy making."

9. (2023) Following criticism that he had not yet bothered to view the refugee crisis he created by opening the floodgates on the Mexican border, Joe Biden spends three hours on a sanitized, "highly controlled" visit to the southern border. The day prior to Biden's visit Border Agents and local cops reportedly cleared El Paso's streets of migrants who'd camped out because the city's shelters were filled beyond capacity. They reportedly even sent many back over the border to Mexico. Ultimately, Biden goes to a processing center where no migrants are present. A senior administration told CNN that to everyone's amazement, "There just weren't any at the

center when Biden arrived. Completely coincidental! They haven't had any today!"

10. (2021) GoFundMe announces it will no longer allow people to fundraise for travel expenses used for potentially violent political events after pro-Trump protesters used the platform to rake in cash ahead of storming the US Capitol. The company will "continue to remove fundraisers that attempt to spread misinformation about the election, promote conspiracy theories and contribute to or participate in attacks on US democracy," their spokesperson announces. The platform doesn't foresee changes relating to raising money to transport violent BLM and ANTIFA members to any location they desire.

11. (2021) Displaying nerves of steel Joe Biden says, "I'm not afraid of taking the oath of office on the West Front of the US Capitol," following the Jan 6 demonstrations that took place there on Jan 6. The fact that the Pentagon has authorized 15,000 National Guard troops to monitor the event may have played a factor in Biden's show of courage.

12. (2023) Joe Biden confirms that a second batch of classified documents has been found in the garage of his Wilmington Delaware home, but he reassures investigators (and the American people) they were secure because the garage also stores his prized Corvette and was "locked." Biden's embarrassment initially threatens to undermine his case against President Trump for his own hoarding of secret material. As time passes, Biden's DOJ will indict President Trump on 37 counts including 31 counts of the Espionage Act alone, which carry a prison term of up to 10 years each, and some obstruction of justice laws carrying up to 20 years each. The DOJ files zero charges against Joe Biden for having done worse.

Republicans and the American people have the audacity to suggest that President Trump is being treated unfairly and raise questions about the "two-tiered" Biden Justice Dept in which Joe and son Hunter constantly receive special treatment under the law.

13. (2022) Disneyland Paris unveils Minnie Mouse's new outfit via Twitter, announcing that Minnie has undergone a high-fashion makeover in honor of its 30th anniversary. The iconic Minnie's new ensemble features a blue polka-dot blazer with matching pants. Stella McCartney also replaced the nearly 100-year-old character's famous red bow with a blue one and swapped her beloved yellow pumps for a pair of black shoes. However,

Minnie's progressive touch-up creates a backlash on social media with one person calling it "more woke BS" from the company and another comparing her new outfit to something Hillary Clinton would wear writing, "Way to go Disney, you turned Minnie Mouse into Hillary Clinton!"

14. (2022) The DOD states it is increasing its efforts to find and eliminate extremism within its ranks, particularly among those who espouse White supremacist beliefs, according to two senior defense officials who wanted to underscore the message that the military will not tolerate extremism within the services. The effort, which started long before the riots of last week, has taken on increased urgency after President Trump's mostly peaceful supporters gathered in front of the US Capitol and attempted to exercise their First Amendment rights on Jan 6. "We clearly recognize the threat from domestic extremists, particularly those who espouse White supremacy or White nationalist ideologies," the official said. They swore to protect and serve, and some joined the riot." Lost on Biden's DOJ is the fact that the vets involved in the protests were "protecting and serving" America. Clearly, actual patriotism, love, and loyalty to America will not be tolerated by Joe Biden's DOD.

15. (2018) On Martin Luther King Jr. Day, LeBron James tweeted, "Injustice anywhere is a threat to justice everywhere. Our lives begin to end the day we become silent about things that matter," a mashup of a paraphrase and a quote from the civil rights leader.

LeBron continues to ramble his way through an embarrassing, tone-deaf statement regarding a team executive's pro-Hong Kong tweet that called out the league for its hypocrisy in advocating for "social justice" while refusing to acknowledge business partner China's brutal track record against its own people.

16. (2022) A new feature on the White House's re-launched website contact form allows people to choose their own pronouns, reflecting the new administration's commitment to diversity. The move was instantly applauded by Equality California, the LGBTQ civil rights org which wrote "In this @WhiteHouse we respect pronouns."

Additionally, GLAAD President and CEO Sarah Kate Ellis issued praise in a statement reading, "On Day One, the Biden administration has taken immediate steps to include trans, nonbinary, and gender nonconforming people in the conversation. Pronouns matter and adding inclusive pronouns to a contact form is more than just a demonstration of allyship."

17. (2022) "Faith-based communities have and will likely continue to be targets of violence by both domestic violent extremists and those inspired by foreign terrorists." A letter from FBI Deputy Director Paul Abbate and John D. Cohen, the top intelligence official at DHS warns that faith-based communities will likely remain targets for violence during Joe Biden's first term.

18. (2023) Sen Majority Whip Dick Durbin states that Joe Biden has lost the "high ground" in the political back-and-forth over classified document storage following the discovery of additional material at Biden's home in Wilmington, Delaware. "When that information is found, it diminishes the stature of any person who is in possession of it because it's not supposed to happen," Durbin said. "Whether it was the fault of a staffer or an attorney, it makes no difference. The elected official bears ultimate responsibility." As much as Biden may want to reply, "Who the Hell cares whether it's fair or not, I'm indicting Donald Trump, anyway" he keeps it to himself.

19. (2023) After The San Francisco African American Reparations Advisory Committee, created in 2020 under the city's human rights commission, was tasked to develop a plan to address "the institutional, City sanctioned harm that has been inflicted upon African American communities," the committee recommends an extensive proposal for reparations that includes a one-time payment of $5 million to each eligible Black resident.

The one-time, lump sum payment of $5 million "would compensate the affected population for the decades of harms that they have experienced and will redress the economic and opportunity losses that Black San Franciscans have endured, collectively, as the result of both intentional decisions and unintended harms perpetuated by City policy," the plan states.

20. (1961) "Ask not what your country can do for you, ask what you can do for your country." During his inaugural address, patriotic President John F. Kennedy issued his famous line. It's a shame that they don't make Democrats like that anymore!

21. (2022) In the State Dining Room, Joe Biden and Anthony Fauci warmly greet one another before Biden signs a series of executive actions meant to

combat the pandemic. Fauci reports he has been guaranteed a new approach by Biden stating, "That was literally a conversation I had 15 minutes ago with the President," he said, clearly relieved by the stark warnings he's been trying to convey about the pandemic for months would now come with the support of the White House.

"Feel good Fauci" wastes no time in projecting his trademark dire warning stating, "We are still in a very serious situation," and reminding Americans that we have recently passed a death toll of 400,000 which is historic in a very bad sense."

22. (2021) DOJ prosecutors are forced to formally walk back their assertion in a court filing that said Capitol rioters sought to "capture and assassinate elected officials" on Jan. 6. A federal prosecutor in Arizona asks a magistrate judge to strike the line in a recent court filing about defendant Jacob Anthony Chansley, a man who is alleged to have led some in the crowd in the Capitol breach, choosing not to add that's Joe Biden's job.

The entire chilling line the prosecutors want to omit from their court filing is: "Strong evidence, including Chansley's own words and actions at the Capitol, supports that the intent of the Capitol rioters was to capture and assassinate elected officials in the United States Government." The stunning move comes a few hours after Michael Sherwin, the acting US attorney in Washington, DC held a press conference and begrudgingly admitted there was "no direct evidence of kill and capture teams" during the siege of the Capitol building. We do not want to mislead the court by discussing the strength of any specific evidence" related to his intent, Allison said.

23. (2013) Sec. Hillary Clinton became combative Wednesday at the Senate Foreign Relations Committee hearing on the Benghazi attack, clashing with Sen. Ron Johnson (R., Wis.) over the talking points given to Ambassador Rice, at one point going into histrionics and screaming, "What difference at this point does it make?"

24. (2023) "I cannot put partisan loyalty ahead of national security, and I cannot simply recognize years of service as the sole criteria for membership on this essential committee. Integrity matters more. Speaker of the House Kevin McCarthy writes a letter to House Minority Leader Hakeem Jeffries explaining why he has officially denied seats on the House Intelligence Committee to Dem Reps. Eric Swalwell and Adam Schiff, the former

chairman of the panel. After his connections to a Chinese spy were exposed years ago, Eric Swalwell is finally removed from his dangerous position on the House Intelligence Committee. Swalwell was a vocal and nasty critic of former President Trump, during the same time he was cavorting with Christine Fang (aka Fang Fang), a Chinese spy with ties to the CCP. It is reported that Swawell even allowed her full access to his office.

25. (2021) "I am deeply concerned about ASPR's (Administration for Strategic Preparedness and Response) apparent misuse of millions of dollars in funding meant for public health emergencies like the one our country is currently facing with the COVID-19 pandemic. Equally concerning is how widespread and well-known this practice appeared to be for nearly a decade." An anonymous whistleblower alleges that (the HHS') Office of the Assistant Secretary for Preparedness and Response, misappropriated millions of dollars in federal funds earmarked for vaccine development and other public health matters diverting them to cover expenses incurred by "the removal of office furniture, news subscriptions and other administrative expenses by the agency."

Although the ensuing report by HHS's inspector general doesn't include an exact estimate of how much money was misspent, it "contains evidence that as recently as (fiscal year) 2019, approximately $25 to $26 million" was taken and improperly used for ASPR expenses.

26. (2019) Channeling her best Greta Thunberg, AOC declares man-made climate change will "destroy the planet" in a dozen years if humans do not address the issue, no matter the cost. During an interview at the MLK Now event in NYC honoring Martin Luther King Jr., Ocasio-Cortez tells interviewer Ta-Nehisi Coates, "Millennials and people, you know, Gen Z and all these folks that will come after us are looking up and we're like, "The world is gonna' end in 12 years if we don't address climate change and your biggest issue is how are we gonna' pay for it?"

She references a recent UN-backed climate report that (predictably) determined the effects of climate change to be irreversible and unavoidable if carbon emissions are not reined in over the next 12 years. She also takes a shot at the Trump admin for "abdicating their responsibilities to govern and address the issue." She adds that activists have a "responsibility" to be vocally opposed to the administration and "breathe fire" when necessary.

AOC's shrill voice of doom inspires little more than mass yawning from the informed.

27. (2023) Fresno County DA criticizes Gavin Newsom and declares "he is either ignorant or a liar" following comments by Newsom claiming that Proposition 47, Proposition 57, and Assembly Bill 109 had all helped to reduce crime in the state. Lisa Smittcamp says that Newsom "should be ashamed of himself" and that the laws he praised were, in fact, "not doing anything to stop" crime in the state. Some of the accomplishments Newsom is boasting about include laws requiring gender-neutral displays of children's toys and toothbrushes in large department stores; clearing the way for a nation's first ban on the sale of new gas-powered leaf blowers and lawnmowers; and prohibiting restaurants from handing out ketchup packets and other disposable condiments unless customers ask for them.

28. (2019) Chicago police say they're investigating a suspected racist and homophobic attack against "Empire" star Jussie Smollett by two masked men at about 2:00 am. They report the actor was punched in the face, had an "unknown chemical substance" poured on him and a rope (noose) wrapped around his neck. For good measure, Smollett tells police the two attackers made several references to MAGA as they beat him. Despite the harrowing attack, the doctors who examine Jussie report his condition is "good."

29. (2019) "This despicable act only shamefully reveals how deeply the diseases of hatred, inequality, racism, and discrimination continue to course through our country's veins." "Empire" co-star Grace Byers condemns our racist country following the hate crime perpetuated against Jussie Smollett.

Other stars including Viola Davis, Janelle Monae, and TI also came out with messages of support for Jussie as does his Empire creator Lee Daniels who posted an emotional video on Instagram, saying, "Hold your head up Jussie. I'm with you!"

Comedian Steve Harvey adds, "This is about coming to the aid of another brother that has tasted the brutality of hatred and racism and bigotry!" No apologies to America are issued following the revelation that Smollet orchestrated the incident.

30. (2007) "I mean, you got the first mainstream African-American who is articulate and bright and clean and a nice-looking guy. I mean, that's a

storybook, man." Non-racist" Joe Biden gives a cringe-worthy compliment to candidate Barak Obama. Biden later apologizes and says the remark was "taken out of context."

31. (2023) Senior congressional sources report that, on behalf of the Biden admin, Sec of State Anthony Blinken has renewed a series of sanctions waivers that permit Iran and Russia to cooperate on nuclear work at Iranian enrichment sites. The Washington Free Beacon reveals that although Blinken authorized the waivers on Jan. 31 Congress was not notified of the decision until late on Feb. 3.

Meanwhile, the free world wonders what could possibly go wrong with Biden's facilitating of Iran and Russia's unholy military alliance and partnership in mining uranium for nuclear bombs.

FEBRUARY

1. (2023) Attorneys for Hunter Biden ask state and federal agencies to investigate a computer repair shop owner, Rudy Giuliani, and a number of right-wing political figures involved in disseminating contents of Hunter's infamous laptop, alleging that they committed computer and other criminal violations in their effort to "weaponize" the laptop contents against Father Joe.

The allegations, made in letters to the Delaware Attorney General, the Justice Department's National Security Division, and the IRS mark the first time Hunter and his legal team publicly acknowledged that it was his personal data purported to be found on a laptop left at the Delaware repair shop. However, his legal team said their new outreach does not amount to confirmation of the laptop narrative that has been circulated on the right.

The letters signal a distinct change in strategy by the "First Son" after bringing on new lawyers to help defend him "against an onslaught of attacks from Republicans, who have sought to use his personal struggles with drugs and congressional probes of his business dealings to attack the president," according to his defenders. Perpetual "victim" Hunter also faces an ongoing federal criminal investigation that is focused on tax and gun charges.

2. (2023) In a party line vote; the House approves a resolution, 218-211, to remove Dem Rep. Ilhan Omar from the House Foreign Affairs Committee. Over Democratic cries of hypocrisy and "revenge-seeking," House Republicans strip the lawmaker of a coveted committee assignment, arguing some past comments she made were laced with anti-Semitism.

As a freshman member in 2019, Omar appeared at different points in public and on social media referring to the influence in U.S. politics of money from wealthy Jewish Americans, a common anti-Semitic trope. Omar apologized and the caucus had largely moved on since that point although House Republicans remained concerned about her racist remarks.

"Is anyone surprised that I am being targeted?" Omar complained in an emotional floor speech, attended by large numbers of the House Democratic caucus who peppered her remarks at several points with cheering. "Is anyone surprised that I am somehow deemed unworthy to speak about American foreign policy or that they see me as a powerful voice that needs to be silenced? Frankly, it is expected because when you push power, power pushes back." In their expulsion resolution, Republicans also cite previous criticisms of Omar from leaders within her own party to justify their extraordinary action.

3. (2023) Fox News Digital reports House Judiciary Committee Chairman Jim Jordan has subpoenaed FBI Director Christopher Wray, ordering him to turn over documents and communications related to the FBI's "misuse of federal criminal and counterterrorism resources" to target parents at school board meetings.

The subpoena compels Wray to produce all documents referring to meetings with U.S. attorneys' offices in accordance with Attorney General Merrick Garland's Oct. 4, 2021, memo that directed the FBI to partner with local law enforcement and U.S. attorneys to identify "parental threats at school board meetings against faculty and prosecute them when appropriate."

Additionally, the subpoena demands documents related to the Justice Department's task force that focused on identifying "school board threats," and the FBI's role as a member of that task force.

The subpoena also requires Wray to turn over all documents related to "both formal and informal recommendations" created or relied upon by FBI employees relating to meetings with U.S. attorneys' offices, as well as "all documents and communications referring or relating to the EDUOFFICIALS threat tag."

4. (2021) Rep. Alexandria Ocasio-Cortez is dubbed "Alexandria Ocasio-Smollett" as details emerge that she fabricated her "trauma" from the Capitol riot, given that she was not even at the site of the siege, at the time. In the four weeks since the riot, Ocasio-Cortez has said repeatedly that she feared for her life on Jan. 6, as a result of a "very close encounter" but details emerged revealing she was in her office in the Cannon building not the Capitol building when protestors entered. The building is part of the overall Capitol complex but is not even within the Capitol building itself.

She had been barricaded in her office for hours when a man who turned out to be a Capitol Police officer rushed into her office to direct her to a safer location for lawmakers, but a terrified AOC said the officer had "anger and hostility in his eyes," making her question if he was trying to put her in a "vulnerable situation." Still, she chose to trust him and not "pass judgment."

As one version of events after another collapses the 31-year-old lawmaker seemingly pulls out all the stops becoming emotional and revealing that she was a sexual assault survivor, which caused her to "struggle with the idea of being believed." FYI AOC - you aren't entitled to "being believed" when you are lying!

5. (2018) Gavin Newsom, the front-runner in California's governor's race, says he "learned an enormous amount" from his past admission of sexual transgressions while mayor of San Francisco more than a decade ago, saying, "I applaud women for coming forward" as part of the #MeT00 movement.

In an event sponsored by POLITICO Newsom is questioned about his past scandal and speaks in great detail about bombshell revelations that erupted when he was mayor, the force of which nearly derailed his career. Newsom became the subject of national headlines in February 2007 when it was revealed his "indiscretions" included having an affair with a subordinate, Ruby Rippey-Tourk, who was also the wife of his chief campaign adviser!

6. (2023) House Republicans issued another series of subpoenas as an on-going investigation into the targeted mistreatment of parents who protested "woke" school boards, voicing their disgust over anti-American propaganda being forced upon their children.

7. (2023) The Chinese spy balloon that transited the US earlier this year was able to capture imagery and collect some intelligence from some US military sites, a source familiar with the matter tells CNN. The balloon was able to transmit information back to Beijing in real-time, the source said, and the US government still does not know for sure whether the Chinese government could wipe the balloon's data as it received it, raising questions about whether there is intelligence the balloon was able to gather that the US still isn't even aware of. A US intelligence official downplays the incident claiming that the balloon was not able to gather any more Intel than Chinese satellites orbiting above the sites.

8. (2022) The U.S. Army announces the release of its first Climate Strategy that guides decision-making in response to threats from climate that affect installation and unit sustainability, readiness, and resilience. The strategy directs how the Army will maintain its strategic advantage through deliberate efforts to reduce future climate impacts and risks to readiness and

national security. America's enemies likely celebrate the news that Woke climate strategists rather than Generals are now directing US military policy.

9. (2023) "You don't have a recession when you have 500,000 jobs and the lowest unemployment rate in 50 years!" During an appearance on ABC's "Good Morning America," Treasury Secretary Janet Yellen tells struggling Americans that the US economy is solid! When asked to square Friday's low unemployment numbers with ABC polling that 41% of Americans feel they are worse off since Biden took office, Yellen sidesteps the question completely and alludes to "stress from the pandemic, the economic impact of the war in Ukraine, and inflation."

She later says Biden will be talking about the "strong and resilient" US economy when he addresses Congress Tuesday, highlighting job creation and bipartisan legislation now in the implementation phase. Essentially, Biden will be informing struggling Americans that they are actually doing great, they just don't appreciate all he has done for them.

10. (2020) "You're a lying dog-faced pony soldier." Joe Biden snaps at Madison Moore a young female college student in New Hampshire when she simply asks him, "How do you explain the performance in Iowa, and why should the voters believe that you can win the national election?" Biden earlier admitted he had "suffered a gut punch" in Iowa's Dem caucuses but apparently Madison's question hurt the former VP's feelings and triggered his angry (and rude) reaction.

11. (2023) After being named "Border Czar" by Joe Biden in March, 2021, VP Kamala Harris' effort to tackle the root causes of migration from Central America reportedly yields more than $4.2 billion in private sector commitments from at least 47 companies collaborating across financial services, textiles and apparel, agriculture, technology, telecommunications, and nonprofit sectors. Despite the small fortune at her disposal, the Border Czar reigns over historically high numbers of immigrants (including MS-13 members, Venezuelan prisoners, rapists) pouring into the US from Mexico.

12. (2023) A DHS spokesman announces the department has retained outside counsel to help ensure the Department's vital mission is not interrupted by "the unprecedented, unjustified, and partisan impeachment efforts by some Members of Congress who have already taken steps to initiate proceedings."

Apparently, the DHS only intends to do the work it is paid to do if their demands that Joe Biden not be held accountable for his epic and disastrous border policy failure aren't met. Additionally, the unjustified and partisan impeachment efforts are hardly "unprecedented." They occurred less than 4 years ago. C'mon man!

13. (2023) At a news CCP ministry spokesperson Wang Wenbin claims it is "common for US balloons to illegally enter other countries' airspace and last year alone, American high-altitude balloons have illegally crossed China's airspace more than 10 times without the approval of relevant Chinese authorities." Wang accuses the US of "illegally" flying high-altitude balloons into its airspace more than 10 times since January 2022. For unknown reasons China did not publicize the details of the US "intrusions" until their own balloon was shot down after traversing the US and spying on American military installations.

14. (2023) Gallup and the Knight Foundation release their annual report surveying Americans for insights into how they view the press. Sadly, the results were grim as only 26% of Americans hold a favorable opinion of the news media - the lowest level recorded by the organizations over the last five years.

Perhaps more startling: the report found that 72% of Americans believe national newsrooms are capable of serving the public, but that they do not believe they're well-intentioned. Only 23% said that they believe national newsrooms care about the best interests of their audiences.

Meanwhile, Americans are having more difficulty than ever in determining what to believe. 61% of respondents said the increase in information across the media landscape has made it harder to distinguish bad information from good. This begs the question, "Can delivering the truth be at the heart of a news organization's mission in 2023 if the aim is to not offend those on one end of the political spectrum at a far greater frequency than the other?" The ultimate irony is this story ran on CNN.

15. (2023) Fox News reports Special Presidential Envoy for Climate John Kerry's family discreetly sold their private jet to a New York-based hedge fund following intense criticism of the plane's carbon footprint in light of Kerry's tireless work fighting global warming. The Kerry family's private jet, a Gulfstream GIV-SP, is no longer owned by his family's charter firm Flying

Squirrel LLC., according to Federal Aviation Administration (FAA) registration information reviewed by Fox News Digital. In financial filings submitted since joining the Biden administration, Kerry had reported that his wife Teresa Heinz-Kerry owned a stake worth more than $1 million in the firm.

16. (2023) "There are roughly 1,000 cases of a train derailing every year!" Transportation Secretary Pete Buttigieg downplays the Ohio rail disaster on the same day Republicans show news footage of chemicals spilled in the accident bubbling to the surface of a creek. "While this horrible situation has gotten a particularly high amount of attention, obviously they have levels of severity," Buttigieg says in a clip posted by Yahoo News on Thursday. "Oh I feel much better now," Republican Sen Josh Hawley tweets back sarcastically on the video.

17. (2022) Republican Sen Roger Wicker, a member of the Senate Armed Services Committee, joins ranking member Sen. Jim Inhofe and 10 other Republican members of the committee in releasing data from the DOD outlining military costs and time spent on key elements of Joe Biden's progressive social agenda. According to General Mark Milley, Chairman of the Joint Chiefs of Staff, U.S. service members spent a total of 5,889,082 man-hours on the February 5, 2021, extremism "stand-down" and "Diversity, Equity, and Inclusion" training, including critical race theory, since Biden took office. Milley provided the data in response to a letter from the senators requesting details about the costs and readiness effects of the Administration's progressive social agenda.

18. (2023) CNN reports that records show President Trump tried to call into Fox News after his supporters swarmed the US Capitol on Jan 6, 2021, but the network refused to put him on air, according to court filings from Dominion Voting Systems in its defamation case against the company. The House select committee that investigated the January 6 attack did not know that Trump had made this call, according to a source familiar with the panel's work.

Trump's newly revealed call to Fox News shows some of the gaps in the record that still exist, due to roadblocks the committee faced. January 6, after the Capitol came under attack, President Trump dialed into Lou Dobbs' show attempting to get on air, but Fox executives vetoed that decision claiming, "It would be irresponsible to put him on the air" and "could have impacted a lot of people in a negative way," according to Fox Business Network President Lauren Petterson, whose testimony was cited by Dominion in the new filing.

Dominion's filing questioned why Fox refused the President's request asking, "Why? Not because of a lack [of] newsworthiness. January 6 was an important event by any measure. President Trump not only was the sitting President, but he was also the key figure that day," Dominion lawyers wrote in their legal brief.

Dobbs' show on Fox Business – in which he routinely promoted baseless conspiracies about the 2020 election – was canceled a few weeks after the Jan 6 "insurrection."

19. (2023) China declares a "major and decisive victory" in its handling of the coronavirus outbreak that swept the country in recent months following an abrupt reaction to its "Covid" policy late last year. The CCP's top decision-making body made the assessment during a closed-door meeting presided over by Chinese leader Xi Jinping, in the latest signal the country is seeking to minimize the political fallout from Covid.

The summary also said the group claimed that China had kept the lowest COVID-19 fatality rate in the world – a metric that China's top leadership touted throughout the pandemic, as its lockdowns, enforced quarantines, and border restrictions kept case numbers – and fatalities – low compared with some other major economies. The committee went on to say China has "created a miracle in human history" as it had "successfully pulled through a pandemic," according to a summary published by state-run news agency Xinhua.

20. (2023) White House spokeswoman Karine Jean-Pierre claims Joe Biden is "the best communicator" in the White House, sparking laughter across the Twitter-verse. After being questioned by a reporter about whether Biden is viewed by his team as "equally adept in all settings in terms of communications," KJP insists that the president's communication skills are the best in his administration.

Social media erupted noting Biden has a long history of being lampooned for word flubs and sometimes incomprehensible speech at public events. Some also noted that others in his administration, such as the press secretary herself and VP Harris, are infamous for their own verbal gaffes.

21. (2023) Jennifer Homendy, chair of the National Transportation Safety Board releases a spate of new details about the fiery train derailment that spewed toxic chemicals and wreaked havoc in East Palestine, Ohio. The report states the initial fire started on February 3 when a hot axle heated a Norfolk Southern rail car carrying plastic pellets.

NTSB says in a preliminary report that a total of 38 train cars derailed in East Palestine, near the Ohio-Pennsylvania border. The number included "11 tank cars carrying hazardous materials that subsequently ignited, fueling fires" that damaged a dozen cars that didn't derail. Five of those derailed train cars were carrying 115,580 gallons of vinyl chloride, according to the report. Vinyl chloride can increase the risk of cancer and is highly flammable.

Those five cars "continued to concern authorities because the temperature inside one tank car was still rising," indicating a polymerization reaction which could result in an explosion, the report said. To help prevent a deadly explosion of vinyl chloride, crews released the toxic chemical into a trench and burned it off three days after the derailment.

The new revelations came after residents who have reported health problems since the toxic train wreck lambasted Norfolk Southern's CEO and after calls for Norfolk Southern to buy the homes of residents who don't feel safe. Meanwhile, embattled Transportation Secretary Pete Buttigieg is in no hurry to visit the affected residents cavalierly saying he will travel to Ohio "when the time is right." This is despite a Post analysis of his schedule, indicating he really hasn't been doing much of anything lately.

22. (2023) The Seattle City Attorney's Office agrees to pay $3.65 million to settle a lawsuit filed by businesses disrupted during the (CHOP) Capitol Hill Organized Protests. The amount includes $600,000 in penalties for the deletion of thousands of text messages by the former mayor, police chief and other high-ranking officials.

23. (2023) "So, during Women's History Month, we celebrate, and we honor the women who made history throughout history, who saw what could be unburdened by what had been." VP Kamala Harris delivers a (poignant) word salad at the White House ceremony to mark Women's History Month.

24. (2023) CNN reports thanks to new legislation that is poised to be signed into law by Democratic Governor Tim Walz, the voting rights of thousands of convicted felons in Minnesota are poised to be restored this summer once they leave prison, instead of after they complete parole,

SF26 was passed by the state Senate earlier this week after the House passed its version of the legislation earlier in the month. Both chambers are controlled by Democrats.

"Minnesota families are expecting legislators to develop solutions to reduce record-breaking crime and violence. Instead, Minnesota Senate Democrats are leaving Minnesotans vulnerable by focusing on providing full state privileges and benefits to convicted felons and non-citizens here illegally," Senate Republican Minority Leader Mark Johnson said in a statement following the vote. Obviously, felons represent an important demographic to Democrats.

25. (2021) Seventy-year-old Mr. Potato Head becomes the latest victim of "Cancel Culture" when Hasbro announces they are dropping "Mister" from his title in order to promote "gender equality for modern consumers." Potato Head's relatives report he is distraught over being canceled, and requests cremation at 450 degrees for a minimum of 45-60 minutes.

26. (2023) Scientists around the world issue a dire warning stating that climate change-fueled water shortages will continue to put enormous pressure on food production. Worse yet, a 2019 study determined the climate crisis, coupled with overgrazing from cattle ranching and other human activities, may disrupt the distribution and cultivation of agave, the main ingredient of Tequila. Okay, now you have our attention!

Feb 27 (2023) Lawmakers and other prominent figures tore into Dr. Anthony Fauci after the Energy Department concluded COVID-19 likely leaked from a lab in Wuhan, China, a theory the former White House chief medical adviser repeatedly rejected.

The Energy Department's "low confidence" assessment, included in a recent classified intelligence report sent to the White House and top members of Congress, turned the focus back on Fauci, who retired at the end of last year after more than five decades in government, spending the last 38 years as Director of the National Institute of Allergy and Infectious Diseases.

Fauci, 82, had come under fire from congressional Republicans for defending gain-of-function research coronaviruses at the Wuhan Institute of Virology, from where COVID-19 is believed to have emerged. The doctor threw cold water on the theory in the months after the outbreak, at one point labeling it a "shiny object in an internal email."

28. (2023) In a startling about-face from Joe Biden brushing off the China spy balloon intrusion as much ado about nothing , Secretary of State Anthony Blinken makes clear that the US has no doubt China was seeking to surveil the US via the balloon that was ultimately shot down off the coast of South Carolina earlier this month.

"I can't say dispositively [sic] what the original intent was, but that doesn't matter because what we saw when it was over the United States was clearly an attempt to surveil very sensitive military sites," Blinken said on ABC's "This Week" in a taped interview Saturday.

"The balloon went over many of them. It, in some cases, loitered," he added. "We took measures to protect that information. We took measures to get information about the balloon. And I think we'll know more when we actually get the remains of the suspected Chinese spy balloon," Blinken added.

US officials now claim the Chinese balloon had a payload—or the equipment it was carrying—roughly the size of three buses, and was capable of collecting signals intelligence, and taking photos. The balloon traveled over sensitive sites in Montana, officials have said, but the Administration said it tracked the balloon's path, and worked to minimize its intelligence collection capabilities.

"There's absolutely no doubt in our minds about what the balloon, once over the United States, was attempting to do. And no doubt in our minds about this surveillance balloon program that China has, and again, has been used over more than 40 countries around the world," Blinken concluded.

MARCH

1. (2022) A report reveals The United States has evacuated only about 3% of Afghans who worked for the American government and applied for special visas abandoning an estimated 78,000 Afghan allies in the chaotic aftermath of the August withdrawal. Cadaver-in-Chief Biden called the botched withdrawal an "extraordinary success." Extraordinary, indeed.

The Afghans stuck in the Taliban-ruled country face increasingly desperate circumstances, the report by the nonprofit Association of Wartime Allies asserts. "Their lives have been devastated by being left behind with seemingly no verifiable path to safety," said the group, which helps Afghans who worked for the U.S. government during America's 20-year-long war.

2. (2023) FBI Director Christopher Wray acknowledges that the bureau believes the COVID-19 pandemic was likely the result of a lab accident in Wuhan, China. In his first public comments on the FBI's investigation into the virus' origins during an interview with Fox News, Wray said, "The FBI has for quite some time now assessed that the origins of the pandemic are most likely a potential lab incident in Wuhan."

Wray says in the interview that the FBI has a team of experts who focus specifically on the risk of biological threats that come into the "wrong hands," including by a "hostile nation state." He continues, "You're talking about a potential leak from a Chinese government-controlled lab that killed millions of Americans and that's precisely what that capability was designed for."

Wray states that most details of the FBI's investigation remain classified and that it has been difficult to work with the Chinese government on investigating the pandemic's origin. "I will just make the observation that the Chinese government, it seems to me, has been doing its best to try to thwart and obfuscate the work here and that's unfortunate for everybody," Wray concluded.

China's Ministry of Foreign Affairs immediately pushed back with spokesperson Mao Ning lecturing "that the parties concerned should stop stirring up arguments about laboratory leaks, stop smearing China and stop politicizing the issue of the virus origin." The FBI's bombshell declaration comes after months of assurances from the CDC that absolved the CCP of any wrongdoing by claiming Covid originated naturally.

3. (1993) "Everybody knows I have tougher ethics rules than any other previous president." Bill Clinton

4. (2007) San Francisco Mayor Gavin Newsom issues a proclamation commemorating the 40th anniversary of a studio that produces porn for gay men.

5. (2023) "Ridiculous!" Dr. Jill Biden responds to concerns about Joe Biden's age, dismissing a proposal by Republican presidential candidate Nikki Haley that politicians over age 75 take a mental competency test. Asked if her husband, who would be 82 at his inauguration if re-elected, would consider taking such a test, Dr. Jill responded, "We would never even discuss something like that." Joe wouldn't remember it either way.

Haley, a former US ambassador to the United Nations and twice-elected South Carolina governor, first put forth the proposal when she announced her presidential candidacy last month. Not surprisingly, ancient Sen. Bernie Sanders also slammed the proposal calling it "absurd and ageist!"

6. (2023) In a stunning development coming just days after the US Department of Energy announced that Covid-19 "most likely" originated in Wuhan, China RadarOnline has uncovered evidence showing Dr. Anthony Fauci commissioned the same February 2020 "scientific paper" in an attempt to disprove the theory the virus was leaked from a Wuhan Chinese laboratory.

7. (2023) "When those doors shut, I cried for 30 minutes straight, uncontrollable sobbing, because that's how much we were holding it together for eight years." Melodramatic Michelle Obama recounts her "breakdown" during her and Barack's flight following President Trump's inauguration. Patriotic Americans feel her pain as they have been sobbing uncontrollably for the entire 8 years the Obamas spent betraying America. Buh-bye!

8. (1999) Vice President Al Gore tells Wolf Blitzer that during his service in the US Congress he took the initiative to invent the Internet.

9. (2023) In an extraordinary rebuke The Biden White House lashes out at Fox News host Tucker Carlson calling him "not credible" after he posts previously unseen footage showing Capitol Police Officers posing for photos with protestors and giving them guided tours of the building during the Jan

6, 2021 "insurrection." Carlson, given access to about 40,000 hours of US Capitol security camera footage by Republican House Speaker Kevin McCarthy, aired clips showing the pro-Trump activists as mostly peaceful patriots. Carlson claims that the "footage provides "conclusive" evidence that Democrats and the House select committee that investigated January 6 lied to Americans about the day's events! The footage reveals truth is a virtue that has no place in the Biden administration.

10. (2023) Trump admin CDC Director Robert Redfield tells a Congressional committee Wednesday that his former colleague, Anthony Fauci, and former National Institutes of Health Director Francis Collins froze him out of discussions on COVID-19's origins. The accusation comes during a politically charged hearing of the House Oversight and Accountability Subcommittee on the Coronavirus Pandemic and stoked Republican claims that Fauci in early 2020 promoted the view that an infected animal spread the virus to humans to divert attention from research the U.S. sponsored at China's Wuhan Institute of Virology.

11. (2023) Justice Department reporter Jerry Dunleavy reveals the US left behind more than $7 billion of military equipment in Taliban-run Afghanistan during the disastrous US military withdrawal in August 2021. John Sopko, the Special Inspector General for Afghanistan Reconstruction, details the revelations related to U.S. military equipment that is now in the hands of the Taliban in a report on "Why the Afghan Security Forces Collapsed" a report released in late February.

12. (2023) In a local Boston radio interview in late January, Elizabeth Warren was enthusiastic about President Joe Biden running for reelection but, when asked if Biden should keep Harris as his running mate, she said, "I really want to defer to what makes Biden comfortable on his team." CNN now reports that Liz has called twice to apologize to Kamala and over a month later, Kamala Harris still hasn't called her back.

The incident and its aftermath, different details of which were described to CNN by multiple people close to the Massachusetts senator and people close to the vice president, has fed an ongoing breakdown of accusations and purported misunderstandings. "Pretty insulting," is how one person close to Harris described the feelings of many in the vice president's office and in her wider orbit.

Several people close to Warren said the senator was calling to explain her statement as purely a mistake, a fumbling, unintentional attempt to avoid stepping on a campaign announcement from the president.

A spokesperson for Warren pointed to the statement the senator issued hours after the original interview clarifying what she said, and an additional person close to Warren cited a personal and political relationship that goes back to being the first senator to endorse Harris for Senate and said of her support, "she didn't mean to imply otherwise."

Warren made her case to Harris' chief of staff Lorraine Voles, who returned the senator's call in place of Harris, a source familiar with the callback told CNN. After the trauma "Pocahontas" endured following her phony Native American claims were exposed, perhaps this is a case of "hurt people hurt people!"

13. (2023) Speaking on MSNBC's "PoliticsNation, Manhattan DA Alvin Bragg praises the "professionalism" of his deputies in probing former President Trump's alleged role in a hush-money scheme and cover-up. Bragg states he and his team are focused "on the evidence and the law. We follow the facts. It doesn't matter what party you are, it doesn't matter your background." Bragg's "set" clearly proves he also has a career as a stand-up comic!

14. (2023) "When Pete's two children were born, he took two months maternity leave, whereupon thousands of travelers were stranded in airports, the air traffic system shut down, [and] airplanes nearly collided in midair. I mean, Pete Buttigieg is the only person in human history to have a child and all the rest of us get postpartum depression." Mike Pence jokes about Pete Buttigieg at the Gridiron Club dinner, an event bringing together some of the city's most prominent journalists and the government officials they cover. It traditionally features politicians making jokes about notable Washington figures.

Pence, however, is immediately admonished by the Biden White House which demands he apologize for his remark and declares his joke "homophobic." White House press secretary Karine Jean-Pierre later issued a statement saying the former VP "should apologize to women and LGBTQ people, who are entitled to be treated with dignity and respect."

The entire incident makes us long for 2019, back in the days when people could take a joke.

15. (2023) In an interview Joe Biden calls efforts to restrict transgender rights in Florida "close to sinful" and suggests federal laws should be passed to protect those rights in all states. Some of Florida's unprecedented (evil) measures include attempting to restrict transgender people from competing on sports teams (males in female sports) or using bathrooms that align with their gender identity (having a male student who decides to identify as female one day so he can hang out in the restroom watching your daughter undress and use the facilities).

Worse yet, Florida indicates it will soon enact a measure banning gender-affirming medical care for youth, including barring doctors from prescribing puberty blockers, hormone therapy, and surgeries for patients under 18. Biden didn't specify which rules he found offensive but said that efforts to restrict the rights of trans individuals were "cruel."

In the interview, Biden also affirms his support for same-sex marriage, describing (yet another) epiphany when he was young in which he saw two "well-dressed men" kissing outside an office building in Delaware. "I'll never forget, I turned and looked at my dad. He said, 'Joey, it's simple. They love each other." Does ANYONE believe that actually happened in Scranton, PA in the 1950's??? Also, what is the significance of them being "well dressed?" Only Joe knows and it's probably better to keep it that way.

16. (2023) Chairman James Comer (R-Ky.) releases new evidence of the Biden family's suspicious business transactions: The House Committee on Oversight and Accountability has issued a memorandum revealing new evidence resulting from the investigation into the Biden family's influence peddling and business schemes. Subpoenaed financial records show that from 2015 to 2017, Biden family members - Hunter Biden, James Biden, Hallie Biden, and an unknown "Biden" and their companies collectively received $1.3 million in payments from accounts related to Rob Walker, a Biden family associate.

Notably, on March 1 (2017) less than two months after VP Joe Biden left public office, State Energy HK Limited, a Chinese company, wired $3 million to Rob Walker's company. The next day, the company wired $1,065,000 to a company connected with James Gilliar, another Biden family associate. Afterward, the Biden family received approximately $1,065,000 in payments over a three-month period in different bank accounts. The bank records show that the Biden family received approximately one-third of the money obtained from the China wires.

17. (2008) "I remember landing under sniper fire. There was supposed to be some kind of a greeting ceremony at the airport but instead, we just ran with our heads down to get into the vehicles to get to our base." Hillary Clinton recounts a harrowing experience (that never actually occurred) during her 1996 trip to Bosnia.

18. (2020) The average price of a gallon of gas falls below $2 in nearly a quarter of the country's states, according to AAA. The national average currently stands at $2.19 a gallon - the lowest it's been since early December 2016. That's down 13 cents from a week ago and 36 cents lower than a year ago. This is unprecedented," Tom Kloza, head of energy analysis for the Oil Price Information Service, tells CNN Business.

He adds that he expects that the national average will soon drop between $1.99 per gallon with some states hitting $1 per gallon or less and that the national average price will probably decline further in the next few months, perhaps to between $1.25 to $1.50 per gallon."

Another look back at the prosperity Americans enjoyed under President Trump! Currently, due to Joe Biden's war on fossil fuel, CA gas prices stand at $6.07 per gallon (for regular). Joe did that!

19. (2020) "'Cause it comes from China!" President Trump responds (quite succinctly) to badgering over his use of the term "China virus" during a White House briefing. The President goes on to explain, "I didn't appreciate the fact that China was saying that our military gave it to them. Our military did not give it to anybody. I think saying that our military gave it to them creates a stigma. "I have great love for all of the people from our country, but as you know China tried to say at one point that it was caused by American soldiers. That can't happen. It's not gonna happen, not as long as I'm President. It comes from China!" he concluded.

Note: Hard not to feel nostalgic when harkening back to the days when America actually had a strong, truthful, patriotic President!

20. (2023) Comic book giants DC Comics and Marvel Comics plan to celebrate Pride Month in June by releasing graphic novels celebrating LGBTQ characters. "Marvel's Voices; Pride #1 published June 23, and it is "Marvel's first-ever queer-centered special spotlighting Marvel's growing tapestry of LGBTQ+ characters."

Marvel also promises that a transgender is coming to the Marvel Universe, according to the company.

The DC Pride comic will be 80 pages long and feature many of their recognizable characters fans know and love including Batwoman, Renee Montoya, Alan Scott, Midnighter, Apollo, Extraño, Poison Ivy, and Harley Quinn, according to the comic company. "DC Pride #1 will (also) include full-page profiles of DCTV's LGBTQIA+ characters and the actors who play them," the news release said.

21. (2023) When asked by Republican Senator Marsha Blackburn to define the word "woman" during the second day of her Supreme Court confirmation hearings, nominee Judge Ketanji Brown Jackson defers the question to scientific experts stating, "I can't…I'm not a biologist."

22. (2023) Joe Biden issues the first veto of his presidency, preserving a Labor Department rule that permits fiduciary retirement fund managers to "consider climate change and social criteria when making investments." By vetoing the measure to nix the rule, Biden, right out of the gate, puts current and future American middle-class retirees on notice that he will put his climate change agenda before their welfare and ability to receive the highest possible investment returns to meet their retirement financial needs.

23. (2021) UN Sec-General António Guterres warns that White supremacy, neo-Nazism, and extremism pose an "international threat" and states his belief that US leaders have a "responsibility" to lead in combating the issue. Guterres also offers, "To address the issue, we need to promote our values and invest economically, socially, culturally in social cohesion." He then called for law enforcement and judicial systems to be trained to address these issues and "make sure that those that misbehave are held accountable."

Guterres completes his treatise by denigrating American combat vets warning, "I think there is permanent intercommunication, there are even mechanisms of mutual recruitment, mutual influence and at the same time we see some of these groups recruiting war veterans, recruiting former members of security forces, having weapons, and becoming a threat to our societies, and in the international sense."

Despite Guterres' moronic assessment, American patriots understand the greatest threat to our country and the world comes from him and his fellow reprobates at the UN who espouse this type of anti-American propaganda! Americans also have long understood that we can always count on the UN to be there when they need us!

24. (2021) Joe Biden taps Kamala Harris to lead the White House effort to tackle the migration challenge at the U.S. southern border and work with Central American nations to address the root causes of the problem.

Biden made the announcement as he and Harris met at the White House on Wednesday with Health and Human Services Secretary Xavier Becerra, Homeland Security Secretary Alejandra Mayorkas, and other immigration advisers to discuss the increase in migrants, including many unaccompanied minors, who arrived at the border in recent weeks. Weren't they invited?

In delegating the matter to Harris, Biden is seeking to replicate a dynamic that played out when he served as President Barack Obama's vice president. Obama turned to Biden in his first term to lead the White House effort to draw down U.S. troops in Iraq and oversee implementation of stimulus in response to the Great Recession.

25. (2023) A WSJ Poll reports on the diminishing of the importance of patriotism for Americans citing a poll that noted yet another notable drop in long-held American values that concluded only 38% of those polled in 2023 said "patriotism" is very important, compared to 70% in 1998 and 61% in 2019. Unfortunately, there are no specific statistics tracking the impact America-loathing college professors are having on the startling drop in the figures.

26. (2023) *"The Telegraph Newspaper" (UK)* reveals novels by "Queen of Crime" Agatha Christie have become the latest classic works to be revised to remove racist references and other language that might offend the sensibilities of "modern audiences."

The article reports publisher Harper Collins has edited some passages and entirely removed others from its new digital editions of some of Christie's detective mysteries featuring Hercule Poirot and Miss Marple. The amendments to the books, published between 1920 and 1976, the year of Christie's death, include changes to the narrator's inner monologue. For example, Poirot's description of another character as "a Jew, of course" in Christie's debut novel, *The Mysterious Affair at Styles,* has been stripped out of the new version.

Throughout the revised version of the short story collection *Miss Marple's Final Cases and Two Other Stories,* the word "native" has been replaced with "local," The Telegraph reports. A passage describing a servant as "black" and "grinning" has been revised and the character is now simply referred to as "nodding," with no reference to his race.

Also, in the 1937 novel *Death on the Nile,* references to "Nubian people" have been removed throughout. The Telegraph reports that HarperCollins released some of the reissues in 2020, with more set to be unveiled.

Additionally, CNN reports that Roald Dahl's classic children's books had received similar treatment. The changes to Dahl's books divided fans of his works including *Charlie and the Chocolate Factory* and *James and the Giant Peach,* with some arguing that rewriting classic literature is a form of censorship.

Publisher Puffin responded to the controversy by announcing that it would release two versions - one amended and one classic – to give readers "the choice to decide how they experience Roald Dahl's magical, marvelous stories," in an effort to appease easily offended audiences.

27. (2023) Federal prosecutors tack on a 13th criminal charge against Sam Bankman-Fried, accusing the FTX co-founder of bribing "one or more" Chinese government officials with $40 million worth of cryptocurrency. In the indictment, prosecutors allege that Bankman-Fried sought to pay off Chinese officials in an effort to unfreeze accounts belonging to his hedge fund, Alameda Research. The accounts, which the Chinese government had frozen, held more than $1 billion worth of digital assets, prosecutors say.

28. (2022) "Everyone wants to know: Is Hollywood racist? Is it burning-cross racist? No. It's a different kind of racist. You're damn right Hollywood's racist, but not the racist that you've grown accustomed to. Hollywood is a sorority racist. It's like, 'We like you, Rhonda, but you're not a Kappa.' That's how Hollywood is," Chris Rock weighs in on the #OscarsSoWhite controversy during his monologue. "But things are

changing. We got a black 'Rocky' this year. Some people call it 'Creed', but I call it 'Black Rocky,'" the comedian adds.

29. (2022) "It took place at Trump International Golf Club in West Palm Beach, Florida, on the 7th hole, which was playing 181-yards into a slight wind. I hit a 5-iron, which sailed magnificently into a rather strong wind, with approximately 5 feet of cut, whereupon it bounced twice and then went clank, into the cup!" Much to the chagrin of wannabe Dem golfers, President Trump recounts the resplendent hole-in-one he sank in a tournament over the weekend later adding, "These great tour players noticed it before I did because their eyes are slightly better, but on that one hole only, their swings weren't." Note: It ain't braggin' if you can do it!

30. (2023) "Now it's a little tricky because you have to be very careful, which makes it really hard for comedians, because the beauty of comedy is that we make fun of ourselves, make fun of life. There's a whole generation of people, kids, who are now going back to episodes of *Friends* and find them offensive. There were things that were never intentional and others… well, we should have thought it through – but I don't think there was a sensitivity like there is now." Feeling a bit out of step with the times, Jennifer Aniston touches on how much the culture has changed since *Friends* debuted in 1994.

Additionally, the show's "lack of diversity" has long been criticized to the extent that series co-creator Marta Kauffman has expressed remorse about it telling the LA Times, "Admitting and accepting guilt is not easy. It's painful looking at yourself in the mirror. I'm embarrassed that I didn't know better 25 years ago." In her defense, it was practically impossible to predict whiny, intolerant, Woke leftists who are offended by anything and everything would ultimately rule America.

31. (2023) According to figures released by his campaign former President Donald Trump raises more than $4 million in the 24 hours after news of his indictment in Manhattan becomes public. The Trump campaign reports that more than 25% of the donations came from first-time donors to the former president, "further solidifying President Trump's status as the clear frontrunner in the Republican primary."

APRIL

1. (2017) Less than two months after Vice President Joe Biden leaves public office, State Energy HK Limited, a Chinese company, wires $3 million to Hunter Biden business associate Rob Walker's company. The next day, the company wires $1,065,000 to a company associated with James Gilliar, another Biden family confidant. Later, the Bidens received $1,065,000 in payments over 3 months deposited in different bank accounts.

2. (2023) According to an investigation by the Information Commissioner's Office, British TikTok allowed up to 1.4 million UK children under the age of 13 to use the platform in 2020 without parental consent. Furthermore, it's discovered the children's data may have been used to track and profile them. The video-sharing site is fined £12.7m by the UK's data watchdog. TikTok protests claiming it has "invested heavily" to stop under-13's from accessing the site.

3. (2023) Proving they have learned absolutely nothing from Lori Lightfoot's reign of terror, Chicagoans elect ultra-ultra-left-wing Brandon Johnson as their next Mayor. Criminals and thugs reportedly rejoice at the news as they excitedly plan to unleash the next wave of violent sprees.

4. (2023) Former President Trump slams Manhattan District Attorney Alvin Bragg from Mar-a-Lago, just hours after pleading not guilty to falsifying business records related to alleged hush-money payments made ahead of the 2016 presidential campaign. President Trump tells supporters, "I never thought anything like this could happen in America."

5. (2023) Adult film star Stormy Daniels is ordered to pay Donald Trump's attorneys an additional $120,000 in legal fees (in addition to the $500,000+ she's previously been ordered to pay). Daniels sued Trump in 2018 alleging, "an unknown man threatened her in a parking lot to keep quiet about their alleged affair." Trump calls the suit "a "total con job."

6. (2023) The State University System of Florida Board of Governors bans TikTok from use on university-owned devices "due to the continued and increasing landscape of cyber threats." The memo states the ban is effective immediately.

7. (2023) Former NCAA swimmer Riley Gaines is forced to barricade herself in a room at San Francisco State University after being physically

assaulted following a speech to students about saving women's collegiate sports. "The prisoners are running the asylum at SFSU! I was ambushed and physically hit twice by a man wearing a dress," Gaines Tweeted later.

8. (2022) New York Magazine reveals BLM founder, Patrisse Cullors, spent $6 million in donated funds on a luxurious Studio City estate in LA. The all-cash deal closed 5 months after George Floyd's death sparked nationwide donations to BLM chapters (including more than $90 million in February alone). Cullors is reportedly at a loss for words when asked to explain how her extravagant purchase of the mansion benefitted any black people's lives.

9. (2023) In the latest exhibition to feature Hunter Biden's artwork, 3 of his paintings (priced at $85,000 apiece) are put on display at a Manhattan art gallery. Priced up to $500,000 Hunter's sales have raised ethical questions and triggered a Republican investigation. Gallerist, Georges Bergès scoffs at the suggestion that a Hunter Biden work could be used to buy political influence, saying, "You could buy a politician for a lot less than that."

10. (2023) A CNN poll states that just one-third of Americans say Joe Biden deserves to be reelected. Meanwhile, The Manhattan Grand Jury indictment of former President Donald Trump triggered a massive surge in donations to his re-election committee, donated courtesy of Americans sickened by Biden's political persecution of the former President.

11. (2023) "People were crying!" In his first interview since his arraignment, former president Donald Trump describes the scene inside the New York City courthouse on "Tucker Carlson Tonight." Those shedding tears across the country reportedly included Lady Liberty, the American Bald Eagle, and every heartbroken patriot who was forced to witness New York's Supreme Court murder of the First Amendment of the US Constitution.

12. (2023) "Evidence suggests that Biden officials and the DOJ unlawfully abused their power and then lied about it to the American people. This government, it seems, acknowledges no limits on its power to harass, intimidate, and silence its political opponents." America First Legal makes a statement after obtaining internal government documents proving the Biden Admin lied when they claimed they only learned about the FBI raid of President Trump's Mar-a-Lago home when viewing it on social media.

13. (2008) "You go into these small towns in Pennsylvania and, like a lot of small towns in the Midwest, the jobs have been gone now for 25 years and nothing's replaced them. And they fell through the Clinton administration, and the Bush administration, and each successive administration has said that somehow these communities are gonna regenerate and they have not. And it's not surprising then they get bitter, they cling to guns or religion or antipathy toward people who aren't like them or anti-immigrant sentiment or anti-trade sentiment as a way to explain their frustrations." Barak Obama expresses his contempt for the 2nd Amendment, religion, and patriotic Americans.

14. (2023) "See this tie I have, this shamrock tie? It was given to by one of these guys right here, who's a hell of a rugby player who beat the hell out of the Black and Tans." While in Ireland Joe Biden confuses the Black and Tans, a brutal force deployed against rebels during the Irish War of Independence with New Zealand's All Blacks rugby team.

15. (2008) "We like Mr. Obama, and we hope that he will win the election." Hamas's top political adviser, Ahmed Yousef, gives the terrorist organization's official endorsement to presidential hopeful Barak Obama.

16. (1998) "Close the door. She'll be in here for a while." Retired Secret Service agent Louis Fox testifies before a federal grand jury as to his orders from Bill Clinton during a White House visit by Monica Lewinsky.

17. (2020) Rebuffing then-President Donald Trump, pathological truth-avoider Dr. Anthony Fauci downplays the possibility of a lab leak triggering the Covid Pandemic, saying "the virus' "mutations are totally consistent with a jump of a species from an animal to a human."

18. (2022) A staffer dressed as the Easter Bunny whisks Joe Biden away from addressing a reporter during the Easter celebration on the White House lawn.

19. (2023) Sen Ted Cruz states Democrats are using Sen Dianne Feinstein as a "sacrificial lamb" and are trying to remove her because she's not "woke" enough. Cruz points out that Feinstein has been attacked by the left for being too respectful to Republicans, such as when she hugged Lindsey Graham after the confirmation hearing of Justice Amy Coney Barrett.

20. (2023) Just the News reports a letter sent to Congress by Atty Mark Lytle on behalf of his client, an IRS agent turned whistleblower in the Hunter Biden tax fraud case, states the agent is willing to provide specific details regarding the criminal tax charges case against Hunter. The letter states that the IRS agent has witnessed "preferential treatment and politics" being used by the DOJ to block any serious attempt to criminally prosecute HB. If revealed to be true, this would prove Attorney General Merrick Garland lied under oath when he claimed that the DOJ had no involvement in the probe against Hunter, which he stated was being left entirely up to Weiss's office.

21. (2023) Joe Biden vows to give at least $1 billion of American taxpayers' money to the United Nations "Green Climate Fund" (GCF) despite the fact the fund has sent millions of dollars to the Communist Chinese Party in the past.

22. (2023) The Washington Beacon reveals visitor records show TikTok lobbyists visited the Biden White House at least 40 times in the past year as part of a plan to rehabilitate their image. TikTok and its parent company reportedly spent over $13 million on federal lobbying since 2019. One such lobbyist, John Breaux, is a former U.S. Senator from Louisiana and a Democrat who visited the White House at least three times in 2022.

23. (2023) A federal judge denies Manhattan District Attorney Alvin Bragg's request for a court order to prevent the House Judiciary Committee from questioning a former prosecutor involved in the investigation of Donald Trump. The court's 25-page order eviscerates the Manhattan DA and his former prosecutor, Mark Pomerantz.

24. (2021) LeBron James deletes a tweet seemingly designed to incite violence against a heroic Columbus, Ohio police officer who was forced to shoot a teenage girl who was attacking another young girl with a knife. James tweeted a photo that appeared to show the officer who was involved in the shooting with the caption: "YOU'RE NEXT #ACCOUNTABILITY."

The body-worn camera of police Officer Nick Reardon clearly shows someone trying to stab a person on the ground. The incident proves that you don't have to be smart (or honest) to become the leading scorer in NBA history.

25. (2023) House Judiciary Committee reveals that the Biden campaign reached out to Michael Morrell, a former Deputy Director of the CIA, to orchestrate an infamous letter on behalf of 51 intelligence officials claiming the *New York Post*'s Hunter Biden laptop story from October 2020 was "Russian disinformation."

26. (2023) Don Lemon is fired by CNN after 17 years of controversy including his most recent remark that Nikki Haley "isn't in her prime because a woman is considered to be in her prime in her 20s and 30s, and maybe 40s." Lemon later apologizes calling his comments "inartful and irrelevant."

27. (2020) "I keep trying to see Chuck Schumer's and Nancy Pelosi's point of view, but I can't seem to get my head that far up my ass!" LA Sen John Kennedy

28. (2007) Hillary Clinton addresses critics who suggest that she had used a fake Southern accent during a stop in Greenville, South Carolina saying she views her "sometimes Southern accent as a virtue."

29. (2023) The body of 22-year-old Spc. Bishop Evans, a Texas National Guard member who went missing three days earlier, is found and identified. Evans drowned while attempting to rescue two migrants who were struggling as they tried to cross the Rio Grande at El Paso. Both migrants are later arrested and charged with illicit narcotics trafficking.

30. (2002) "You just wonder if she shouldn't start at home with this crusade." Juanita Broaddrick, commenting on Hillary Clinton's new anti-rape legislation. Broaddrick claimed she was raped decades prior by then-Governor Bill Clinton.

MAY

1. (2023) "Borrowers don't just need their debts paused; they need them erased." Sen Majority Leader Chuck Schumer beseeches Joe Bidden to use executive action to cancel $50,000 in student debt for each borrower. Erasing college student debt remains a top priority for leftists who believe being taught to hate America in college should be free.

2. (2023) Chanting "trans rights are human rights," leftist insurrectionists storm the Texas State Capitol to protest SB 14 a bill that seeks to ban gender reassignment surgeries for children. House Speaker Dave Phelan is forced to order the state police to clear the gallery so proceedings can resume. Outside rioters assault a woman who supports the state legislature's efforts to protect children.

3. (2023) Sen Bob Menendez (D-NJ) blasts Biden's decision to send troops to the border declaring, "There is already a humanitarian crisis in the Western Hemisphere, and deploying military personnel only signals that migrants are a threat that requires our nation's troops to contain. Nothing could be further from the truth." MS-13 gang members, terrorists, and convicted pedophiles arrested while trying to enter the US aside, Menendez may have a point.

4. (2023) NY Post reports that the IRS has been stockpiling $10 million worth of ammo, weapons, and combat gear since 2021 to ramp up the militarization of its agents. The jaw-dropping figure includes $2.3 million on ammo, $1.2 million on ballistic shields, $474,000 on Smith & Wesson rifles, $463,000 on Beretta tactical shotguns, and $243,000 on body armor.

5. (2023) The Republican-controlled legislature of Florida passes several bills cracking down further on forced "diversity" in public schools including requiring students and teachers alike to use someone's "preferred pronouns." One of the bills also bans classroom instruction on sexuality until the 8th grade.

6. (2004) Nineteen of twenty-three officers who served with John Kerry in Vietnam declare Kerry "unfit to be commander-in-chief."

7. (2023) "They make me vomit!" In a PBS interview with Margaret Hoover, actor Richard Dreyfuss responds to a question as to his feelings on

the Academy Awards' newly implemented "diversity guidelines," stating movies must meet certain criteria for representation to be eligible for the Academy Award for Best Picture. Films have to meet at least two of four benchmarks, which cover (among other things) whether the lead actors are from underrepresented groups or if at least 30% of the cast and crew come from those groups.

Dreyfuss reports his frustration is because movies are "an art and no one should be telling me as an artist that I have to give into the latest, most current idea of what morality is." The inclusion standards were enacted in an attempt to address inequality in the industry, which gave rise to the #OscarsSoWhite movement in 2015. Can you say "canceled?" Yes, he was.

8. (1991) At the Little Rock Excelsior Hotel in Arkansas, Bill Clinton (allegedly) exposes his penis to Paula Jones and asks her to perform fellatio.

9. (2023) Court documents reveal the FBI misused FISA 278k times in 2020-2021.

10. (2023) The Biden admin seemingly classifies middle-aged pro-life mothers as "domestic terrorists" due to their opposition to abortion.

11. (2023) "Why would any leader put our Black communities already riddled with crime, at further risk by placing unvetted, non-taxpayers steps away from our seniors, our children, and our homes we've worked so hard on our own to secure?" A Chicago resident vents during a Fox 32 news segment covering the arrival of a busload of migrants at Windy City South Shore High School.

12. (2022) During her final briefing as White House press secretary, Jen Psaki thanked her press office colleagues and members of the media, telling them, "Thank you for making me better," begging the question, "Better than what?"

13. (2020) Former VP Joe Biden defends his record of helping African Americans and advancing civil rights and voting rights, before ending an interview by telling a black radio host "If you can't decide whether to vote for Biden or Trump, you ain't black!"

14. (2023) "He's like Clarence Thomas, a Black Republican who believes in pulling yourself up by your bootstraps, rather than, to me, understanding the systemic racism that African Americans face," Joy Behar declares neither Tim Scott nor Clarence Thomas understand what it's like to be Black in America the way she does.

15. (2023) Squad members Cori Bush and Rashida Tlaib are the only two House lawmakers to vote against a resolution that recognizes law enforcement officers killed in the line of duty, arguing the measure is "intended to advance Republicans' false narrative."

16. (2023) After spending two years denying that his immigration policies have created a border crisis, Joe Biden finally admits there's a big problem and announces he is sending 1,500 U.S. troops to the Mexican border to support Border Patrol agents ahead of an expected surge of up to 1 million illegal additional migrants once he allows Title 42 to end in a few days.

17. (2023) Gov. Gavin Newsom reports California's budget deficit has ballooned to $32 billion. Despite having a $306 billion budget, by far the largest state budget in the nation, Cali (under Newsom's stewardship) is one of the only states to have a shortfall in 2023.

18. (2023) The Daily Mail reports Cori Bush has called for the US to increase the federal debt by roughly 40% in order to cover $14 trillion in reparations to compensate African Americans for slavery. The money is reportedly designed "to bridge the black and white wealth gap."

19. (2023) Sam Brinton, flamboyant LGBTQ activist and former Joe Biden Deputy Assistant at the Office of Nuclear Energy, is arrested for the third time on charges related to baggage theft, this time at Washington National Airport.

20. (2023) The Daily Wire reports the "Hillary for America PAC" (run by longtime pro-Clinton operative David Brock) stands accused of violating the very campaign finance laws that were enacted by her and Democrats to cut back on "the influence of big money in politics."

21. (2023) It's reported that on April 21 and 22, Princeton University's Lewis Center for the Arts hosted a play entitled, "To All The Babies I've Killed Before: A Love/Hate Letter To Storytelling." The play reportedly focuses on "abortion, womanhood, queerness, and identity."

22. (2023) Washington Post reports officials now say they "are no longer confident we killed a senior AQ official" and are offering a slightly different view stating, "though we believe the strike did not kill the original target, we believe the person to be al-Qaeda."

23. (2023) "Florida is openly hostile toward African Americans, people of color, and LGBTQ+ individuals. Before traveling to Florida, please understand the state 'devalues and marginalizes the contributions of, and the challenges faced by African Americans and other communities of color.'" The NAACP issues a travel advisory for Florida citing Governor Ron DeSantis' "aggressive attempts to erase Black history and to restrict diversity, equity, and inclusion programs in Florida schools."

24. (2022) Grandstanding Texas gubernatorial candidate, Beto O'Rourke, bursts into a press conference and chastises TX Republican Governor Greg Abbott following the deadly shooting at the Uvalde elementary school.

25. (2023) "This government will crush you and your family if you try to expose the truth about things, they are doing that are wrong." Before a committee investigating the weaponization of the FBI, Special Agent Garrett O'Boyle describes experiencing "retaliatory conduct" and testifies the Bureau "is engaging in a purge of agents who hold conservative beliefs."

26. (2022) House Republicans hold a hearing featuring testimony from parents who say their decision to speak up at school board meetings resulted in a DOJ effort to intimidate and silence them. A DOJ memorandum from Atty Gen Merrick Garland issued to address an alleged "spike in harassment, intimidation, and threats of violence at school board meetings," confirms the parent's claims.

27. (2022) "As we prepare to celebrate Pride Month in a few days, I am excited to announce this historic change that represents another victory in our fight to help ensure equality and respect for the LGBTQ+ community." NY Governor Kathy Hochul celebrates the passage of "The Gender Recognition Act," which enables NY residents to choose an "X" marker for their gender on state identification cards. Progressivism at its finest.

28. (2021) Leaked documents reveal Walt Disney World is implementing "Reimagine Tomorrow," a new anti-racism, diversity, and inclusion training

program that will require park employees to complete a "privilege assessment" and encourage staff "to take ownership of educating themselves about structural anti-Black racism" and asks white employees to "work through feelings of guilt, shame, and defensiveness to understand what is beneath them and what needs to be healed."

29. (2023) Critics rip Disney for allowing, "Nick," a mustachioed male employee wearing a dress and make-up to sell princess dresses to little girls at Disneyland's "Bibbidi Bobbidi Boutique." Nick introduces himself to the young girls as "one of the fairy godmother's apprentices."

30. (2022) Nancy Pelosi's husband, Paul (82) is arrested for DUI after being involved in a collision. When asked by officers to present his driver's license, a slurring Pelosi flashes his "CHP 11-99" credentials in a clear attempt to obtain "preferential treatment." Days later his membership with the police charity is cancelled.

31. (2017) While in London Robert De Niro is quoted as saying, "that if the US was a movie today it would now be a "tragic, dumb-ass comedy." America responds to DeNiro telling him "tragic dumbasses comedies shouldn't throw stones!"

JUNE

1. (2023) While preparing to bound off the stage after handing out the last diploma at the Air Force Academy's commencement ceremony, Joe Biden trips over a sandbag. The moment is captured on video and is viral before the White House has a chance to get ahead of the story. Unnamed sources claim Biden cursed and said, "C'mon, man! I'm not senile just accident prone!"

2. (2023) "America is a land of opportunity, not a land of oppression. When grandfather's journey. He was born in 1921 in the Jim Crow south and watched his family go from cotton to Congress in his lifetime."
Sen Tim Scott.

3. (2023) Trump admin CDC Director, Robert Redfield, tells a congressional committee investigating COVID-19's origins that Anthony Fauci prevented him from presenting Republicans' beliefs that China's Wuhan Institute of Virology was Ground Zero for the pandemic.

4. (2023) The BabylonBee reports the classified documents recovered from the FBI raid on President Trump's Mar-a-Lago home include McDonald's secret recipe for its "McRib" sandwich.

5. (2021) "Why are we giving American tax dollars to countries that hate us? They should be able to hate us for Free!" Sen John Kennedy

6. (2022) According to media reports the CDC tells NBC News that more than 82 million Covid 19 vaccine doses have gone to waste since the beginning of the pandemic. That's in addition to the 65 million-plus doses AP reported were wasted in February.

7. (2023) "President Biden has hijacked PEPFAR, the $6 billion a year foreign aid program designed to mitigate HIV/AIDs in many targeted (mostly African) countries in order to promote abortion on demand."

Bad actor nongovernment organizations that promote abortion have received at least $1.34 billion from PEPFAR funds." In a letter to Congress, Senator Christopher Smith details his disgust with Joe Biden's looting of money meant to help poor AIDS-ravaged nations and diverting it to promote abortion.

8. (2020) "I don't know where you live Jesse but in my state, the price of gas is so high it would be cheaper to buy cocaine and just run everywhere." Sen John Kennedy remarks on the soaring price of gasoline during an interview with Jesse Watters.

9. (2021) "And I haven't been to Europe. And I mean, I don't … understand the point that you're making." During a contentious interview with NBC's Lester Holt "Border Czar," Kamala Harris defends her refusal to actually visit Joe Biden's open southern border.

10. (2023) "In the end, they're not coming after me. They're coming after you - and I'm just standing in their way." Following his "historic" (and baseless) indictment, President Trump addresses a jammed Columbus Convention Center audience regarding the dangers of Biden's Deep State. Many attendees carried signs reading "The FBI is the DNC for the KGB!"

11. (2023) Dem Sen Caroline Menjivar introduces CA bill (SB729) which "demands insurance companies bear the full burden of surrogacy costs for same-sex couples longing for parenthood" and expands the meaning of "infertility" to "encompass situations where individuals or couples cannot conceive without the aid of legislature."

12. (2020) "American policing has never been a neutral institution. The first U.S. city police department was a slave patrol and modern police forces have directed oppression and violence at Black people to enforce Jim Crow, wage the War on Drugs, and crack down on protests." Ignoring proof that lack of officers has the most devastating effects on minority communities, the ACLU campaigns for defunding the police.

13. (1996) "We must take seriously this threat of older men who prey on underage women. There are consequences to decisions and, one way or the other, people always end up being held accountable for their actions." Bill Clinton makes an impassioned speech aimed at fighting teen pregnancy.

14. (2023) Following his arraignment on his most recent indictment President Trump states, "It's no coincidence these charges against me came down the very same day House Republicans reviewed a document tying Joe and Hunter Biden to a $5 million bribery scheme involving Ukraine Energy Co. Burisma."

15. (2023) The Democrat-led Senate Judiciary Committee holds an oversight hearing to examine Section 702 of the Foreign Intelligence Surveillance Act (FISA). This is the tool the FBI used to criminally fabricate the Trump-Russia collusion hoax so Dems are big fans.

16. (2023) With a heavy police and security presence along the first level of seating, the Sisters of Perpetual Indulgence, a LGBTQ activist group, are honored with the Los Angeles Dodgers' community hero award on the team's Pride Night. Probably not the best ambassadors for "America's past time."

17. (2023) NY Post reports the FBI informant in Joe Biden's alleged role in the Burisma bribery scheme claims the Ukrainian businessman who reportedly paid off the former VP has 15 audio recordings of Hunter Biden and 2 of Joe Biden interacting with Burisma's Board of Directors beginning in 2014.

18. (2023) In video footage from a White House event, Eva Longoria is shown fighting off Joe Biden as he clings to her and attempts to fondle her breasts.

19. (2023) "The state of Florida never provided medically necessary gender-affirming care to Duane Owen, causing her enormous suffering and violating her right to be free from cruel and unusual punishment." The ACLU laments the suffering over gender dysphoria endured by convicted pedophile and murderer Duane Owen who was recently executed by the state.

20. (2022) Data from the DOD detailing military costs and time spent on Joe Biden's progressive social agenda are released. According to Gen Mark Milley, the military spent 5,889,082 man-hours on the February 5, 2021 "Diversity, Equity, and Inclusion" training, including critical race theory, at Biden's behest. Judicial Watch President Tom Fitton states in a press release "Our military is under attack – from within."

21. (2023) "I'm not being cynical about Tim Scott individually, but I am maybe suggesting his rhetoric of can't we all get along has to be undergirded with an honest accounting of our past and our present." Barak Obama frets over the prospect of America electing a non-race baiting, honest, patriotic Black president who doesn't fan the flames of racism the way Obama did during his 8-year presidency.

22. (2023) "I don't think the leadership knew where it was and knew what was in it and knew what was going on. "I think it was more embarrassing than it was intentional." Joe Biden rushes to defend both his incompetence and the Communist Chinese Party in the wake of the Chinese spy balloon controversy.

23. (2023) Washington Free Beacon reports that an IRS whistleblower who worked on the Hunter Biden tax probe, tells members of the House Ways and Means Committee that Hunter Biden improperly deducted tens of thousands of payments to a hooker and a Sex Club on his 2018 taxes.

24. (2022) House Republicans hold a hearing featuring testimony from parents who say their decision to speak up at school board meetings has resulted in a DOJ effort to intimidate and silence them. Much of the focus is on Merrick Garland's recently issued memo alleging a "spike in harassment, intimidation, and threats of violence at school board meetings. Unsaid in the memo is that only the Biden Admin can use "harassment, intimidation and threats of violence" against American citizens.

25. (2023) Shellyne Rodriguez, 45, who was recently fired from Hunter College after cursing out pro-life students and threatening a Post reporter by putting a machete to his neck, claims she's the actual victim, arguing the college has "capitulated" to racists and misogynists by terminating her.

26. (2023) "The woke-a-- idiots who run this city are doing everything in their power to destroy it." In a one-man protest of NY City's regulation to cut carbon emissions by banning pizza ovens, Conservative artist, Scott LoBaido, lobs several cheese pies across the NY City Hall fence.

27. (2022) MSNBC political commentator, Keith Olbermann, furiously reacts to the Supreme Court's decision regarding New York's concealed carry ruling by ranting on Twitter that SCOTUS should be ignored and dissolved completely. Once a respected ESPN sportscaster, Olbermann remains afflicted with an incurable case of "Trump Derangement Syndrome." You remain in our prayers, Keith.

28. (2023) After the nation's "report card" shows American children were devastated by the Covid school lockdowns promoted by teacher unions, Joe Biden honors the ineptitude of former American Federation of Teachers

Union boss, Randi Weingarten, by appointing her to a Department of Homeland Security School safety advisory committee.

29. (2021) Marine Veteran Daniel Penny is charged in the chokehold death of a homeless black man on a NY subway. After shouting and threatening passengers on the subway, Penny stepped up to defend the vulnerable. For his trouble, he plead "not guilty" to charges of criminally negligent homicide and second-degree murder. If convicted, he faces a 4-year sentence.

30. (2023) "Well I think, culture is, is a reflection of our moment and our time. Right? And, and, and present culture is the way we express how we're feeling about the moment, and we should always find times to express how we feel about the moment. That is a reflection of joy. 'Cause you know … it comes in the morning." VP Kamala Harris eloquently defines "culture while in attendance at the Essence Magazine "Festival of Culture" in New Orleans.

JULY

1. (2022) NY Post article reveals that 8 months after Hunter Biden's first art opening, Joe Biden appoints Democrat donor, Elizabeth Hirsh Naftali, to the prestigious US Commission for the Preservation of America's Heritage Abroad. Naftali is reportedly among the buyers of Hunter's canvases, some of which commanded $500,000 each.

2. (2017) New Jersey Governor Chris Christie is photographed with his hands folded over his belly, surrounded by his sunbathing family while enjoying a beautiful private beach day on the 4th of July weekend at Island Beach State Park, which was closed to the public due to Covid.

3. (2023) Vermont Native American Indian Chief says Ben & Jerry's headquarters sits on "stolen' land" calling out the hypocrisy in the company's July 4 tweet that America was founded on land stolen from Native Americans.

4. (2023) Border Patrol agents on the Canadian and Mexican borders release a statement that 127 noncitizens listed on the FBI's terror watchlist have been apprehended while trying to enter the US illegally.

5. (2023) The CDC website publishes an article on "Chestfeeding" for transgender, trans-identified, and non-binary gendered individuals "who may give birth and breastfeed or feed at the chest." The CDC article states, "The gender identity or expression of transgender individuals is different from their sex at birth. The gender identity of nonbinary-gendered individuals does not fit neatly into either man or woman. An individual does not need to have given birth to breastfeed or chestfeed. Some families may have other preferred terminology for how they feed their babies, such as nursing, chestfeeding, or body feeding." The site also contains updated information on the correct use of "pronouns" as well as how to correctly use "preferred terms" for racial/ethnic groups.

6. (2023) The DOJ has spent over $9.2 million investigating former President Donald J. Trump since the appointment of special counsel Jack Smith (November, 2022), according to the first accounting of expenses into his budget and that of other Justice Department agencies, including $1.93 million spent on the U.S. Marshals who provide the prosecutor with a security detail.

7. (2023) 7 Attorneys General signed a letter blasting Target for pushing the "Pride Month Campaign" on children, pointing out the company "wittingly marketed and sold LGBTQIA+ promotional products to families and young children as part of a comprehensive effort to promote gender and sexual identity among children."

8. (2023) CA Dem, Julia Brownley, introduces "The Amend the Code for Marriage Equality Act," which addresses issues critical to taxpayers such as removing the words "husband" and "wife" from federal law and substituting words with phrases such as "a married couple, married person and person who has been, but is no longer, married to, (depending on the context)." Future changes will refer to pedophiles as "minor attracted."

9. (2023) After passing unanimously in the Senate, Democrats blocked a bill that would render sex trafficking a "felony" in California. CA Dems apparently don't consider kidnapping women and children and forcing them into prostitution any more serious a crime than they do a (misdemeanor) ticket for shoplifting.

10. (2023) In a column titled, "It's Seven Grandkids, Mr. President," Maureen Dowd challenges Joe Biden's image of a devoted family man and doting grandfather, accusing him of "scarring" Navy (son Hunter's estranged 4-year-old daughter with an ex-stripper) by refusing to even acknowledge the little girl's existence."

11. (2023) US women's soccer player Megan Rapinoe says she would "absolutely" support having a trans woman on the USWNT roster, even if that meant replacing a biological female.

12. (2023) In a vomit-inducing moment, View cohost Joy Behar states she is "turned on" by President Joe Biden's reported rage and volatility toward White House staffers.

13. (2023) While reporting on Bud Light's drop in sales following its partnership with trans influencer, Dylan Mulvaney, a CNN correspondent sets off a firestorm when he refers to Mulvaney as 'he" leading to a wave of backlash from leftists on social media over "misgendering."

14. (2023) Video shot on the tarmac at Helsinki shows 80-year-old Joe Biden putting his mouth on the shoulder of a little girl, pretending to nibble her. The terrified child, who is being held in her mother's arms, turns away as the scary president sniffs her hair and tries to give her a peck on the head.

15. (2023) "When we invest in clean energy and electric vehicles and reduce population, more of our children can breathe clean air and drink clean water." Kamala Harris delivered a speech at Coppin State University in Baltimore where she described Dems' plans to cut both greenhouse gas emissions, and "the population." Americans pray this is just another Kamala gaffe.

16. (2023) After testifying at a congressional hearing that he never owned a private jet, "Climate Czar" John Kerry is reportedly shocked after flight tracking data obtained by Fox News Digital reveals a Gulfstream GIV-SP jet owned by Kerry's family made a total of 48 trips that lasted more than 60 hours and emitted an estimated 715,886 pounds, or 325 metric tons, of carbon over the course of the Biden admin's first 18 months.

17. (2023) "Squad" member Cori Bush asserts, "The Declaration of Independence was written by enslavers and didn't recognize Black people as human," and goes on to declare, "Today is a great day to demand reparations."

18. (2022) Dr. Jill Biden apologized for her San Antonio breakfast remarks the previous morning in which she compared Latinos to "breakfast tacos!"

19. (2022) "This is another bad example of Nancy Pelosi's leadership, and this isn't the first time that her husband did this. He bought stock options ahead of all the Big Tech hearings. This is another example of the media turning a blind eye to Nancy Pelosi's unethical behavior." James Comer reacts to Nancy Pelosi's history of inside trading.

20. (2023) TikTok reports being "chronically late" to appointments (like work) is now deemed "a medical condition," which is now being called "time blindness." Employees claiming to have the condition insist on having special accommodations put in place to help them fight through their malady.

One TikTok user rocks the boat when he responds, "I have actual blindness and I am always on time!"

21. (2023) Whoopi Goldberg alleges BLM rioters who burned down neighborhoods and destroyed businesses in black communities in the wake of the George Floyd protests were "taking care of their towns."

22. (2017) Governor Chris Christie signs legislation "protecting" transgender students at New Jersey's public schools by enacting a bill prohibiting schools from forcing transgender students to use bathrooms or locker rooms that conflict with their "gender identity." Schools will also be required to make sure transgender students are addressed by the name and pronoun they prefer.

23. (2023) A White House source reveals Joe Biden is making changes to his routine to accommodate his frailty and declining mobility as the 2024 election cycle heats up. Among Biden's changes are wearing sneakers, often without sock, as well as using a shorter set of retractable stairs to board Air Force One.

24. (2023) "President Biden has spent most of his political career working on gun laws, on gun reform. Does he believe that someone who is charged with possessing a firearm illegally should be prosecuted to the fullest extent of the law?" During a press conference, Karine Jean-Pierre repeatedly dodges a reporter's questioning on the hypocrisy of Hunter Biden's firearms charges potentially being dismissed.

25. (2023) NY City agrees to pay violent BLM rioters $13.7 million after being sued over the "mass arrests" following the George Floyd rioting. If approved by a judge, each BLM rioter is eligible to receive a payout of $9,950 as part of the settlement. No mention is made of the harsh treatment being doled out to the Jan 6 protestors who remain imprisoned and face lengthy prison terms for their role in the mostly peaceful protest.

26. (2023) Chris Clark, Hunter Biden's lawyer, admits in court that the president's son received $664,000 from CEFC China Energy Co. in 2017, contradicting President Joe Biden's claim that Hunter never received money from a Chinese entity.

27. (2023) Former U. Penn female swimmer testifies that teammates of Lia Thomas were forced to undergo "re-education" to make them "comfortable with the idea of undressing in front of a male." She states, "My teammates

and I were forced to undress in the presence of Lia, a 6' 4" tall biological male, fully intact with male genitalia, 18 times per week."

28. (2022) HB3751, a bill allowing non-U.S. citizens to become police officers passes in the Chicago state house and senate before being (proudly) signed into law by Dem Gov. J.B. Pritzker. On January 1 (2024), American citizens in the state will be subject to arrest by foreign nationals whose only requirement to obtain a law enforcement position is that they are legally authorized to work in the US under Federal law. Hopefully, MS13 gang members will be encouraged to apply.

29. (2023) The House Judiciary Committee releases files showing Joe Biden's White House aides pressured Facebook to censor Tucker Carlson and a COVID-19 vaccine meme featuring actor Leonardo DiCaprio's character from the film "Once Upon a Time … in Hollywood" as he points at his TV (beer and cigarette in hand) to a caption on the screen reading, "10 years from now you will be watching TV and hear…. Did you or a loved one take the Covid vaccine? You may be entitled…"

30. (2021) In an effort to reassure financially struggling American families the Biden White House issues a tweet that cites a Farm Bureau report declaring the cost of a 4th of July barbeque was down 16 cents from one year ago and touts it as "proof that Biden's economic plan is working." Grateful Americans want to know how to best invest this 16-cent windfall.

31. (2023) CNN's Kasie Hunt asks Joe Biden's former special assistant, Michael LaRosa, why it "took so long" for the Biden's to acknowledge their 7th grandchild?" When LaRosa responds that the little girl is "a very gross and uncomfortable subject to talk about," Hunt pushes back and snaps, "Let's not call a little girl gross."

AUGUST

1. (2022) NBC News journalists are reportedly "vexed and dismayed" upon learning of MSNBC's intention to hire White House Press Secretary Jen Psaki upon her exit from the Biden Administration. Some reporters fretted that she "tarnishes the NBC News brand." An undisclosed source within MSNBC angrily admonished the network declaring, "Look, if there is one thing we don't need any help with, it's tarnishing the news. They won't get any argument from us on that point."

2. (2023) "Eventually this is going to come to a neighborhood near you! We need to control the border, we need to call a state of emergency, and we need to properly fund this national crisis!" Sounding like Conservatives, NYC Mayor Eric Adams calls out the Biden Admin for facilitating the overwhelming influx of tens of thousands of migrants into his "sanctuary city."

3. (2023) "Because if people were reporting the intelligence correctly, if I was allowed to do my job as Chief, we wouldn't be here today. This didn't have to happen. Everything appears to be a cover-up!" In a leaked interview with Tucker Carlson Fox News refused to air, former U.S. Capitol Police Chief, Steven Sund, vents and states the Jan 6 "insurrection" was a "cover-up." He expresses his disappointment in the way former House Speaker Nancy Pelosi and former Joint Chiefs of Staff Chairman Mark Milley handled the intelligence that suggested problems would arise on Capitol Hill on January 6.

"Like I said, I'm not a conspiracy theorist, but when you look at the information and intelligence they had, the military had, it's all watered down. I'm not getting intelligence. I'm denied any support from the National Guard in advance. I'm denied National Guard while we're under attack, for 71 minutes." Sund has more than three decades of experience in law enforcement and served as the Capitol Police chief from 2019 to 2021.

4. (2023) After hundreds of teens invade Chicago's South Loop and loot a convenience store, Chicago Mayor Brandon Johnson snaps at a reporter for referring to the criminals as "mobs" instead of using his preferred terminology of "just large gatherings."

5. (2023) Babylon Bee reports the most advanced Artificial Intelligence on the planet was declared an illiterate moron after viewing CNN for just three

hours. Experts believe the A.I., which scours the Internet for information, could not escape the black hole of idiocy that is CNN's content. Puny humans on the A.I. development team first became aware of a problem when the software began speaking illogically about a variety of topics, much like CNN's Jim Acosta, the Bee concludes.

6. (2023) District Judge Tanya Chutkan, a vocal critic of Donald Trump and who forcefully rejected his attempts to block House select committees investigating January 6 from accessing more than 700 pages of records from his White House is "randomly selected" to preside over the former President's faux "insurrection" trial.

7. (2023) Kelly Barnett, Gold Star mother of Marine Corps Staff Sgt. Darin Hoover, calls Joe Biden and his military leadership "incompetent, cowards, and evil," as the families of the 13 US service members killed in the ISIS suicide bombing during Biden's catastrophic Afghanistan US troop withdrawal gather to express their frustration and contempt for the White House and its complete lack of accountability in their loved one's deaths.

It only got worse when Biden (as always) personalized the tragedy stating, "My wife, Jill, and I know how you feel. We lost our son as well and brought him home in a flag-draped coffin," Biden said as he addressed the gathering. Cheryl Rex, a Gold Star mother whose son Marine Lance Cpl. Dylan Merola died in the bombing recounted, "My heart started beating faster and I started shaking, knowing that their son died from cancer, and they were able to be by his side."

Joe Biden has long falsely claimed Beau died in Iraq despite the fact he passed away in May 2015 at Walter Reed National Military Medical Center in Bethesda, Md. 6 years after he came home from a yearlong deployment to Iraq in September 2009. Beau Biden died of brain cancer on US soil.

Neither Biden nor anyone in his administration has been held accountable for the tragedy that unfolded that horrific day.

8. (2023) "It cannot happen, or we will not be the United States of America. If he were to be president, it would be a criminal enterprise in the White House." NY Magazine quotes Nancy Pelosi's shrill doomsday scenario if President Trump is re-elected. Pelosi made no mention of the Biden Crime Syndicate currently occupying the White House.

9. (2023) "They treat us very well. There's nothing they stop us from doing. They give us good hot food, which is freshly made; the food is very good. Yesterday, I had a chicken cutlet. There is no curfew at the shelter." Immigrant Miguel Mujica tells the NY Post that life is good at the McCarren Play Center in trendy Williamsburg, VA after the city set up 100 military cots there to help take pressure off city shelters bursting at the seams housing migrants.

Mujica reports his wife, 5-year-old daughter, and 15-year-old son live out of a family migrant hotel in Sunset Park, Brooklyn, where he was kicked out for an "undisclosed reason." The asylum-seeker has been enjoying taxpayer-funded amenities such as specially prepared Venezuelan cuisine, free WiFi, and international calls, in addition to the park's massive pool next door.

"I brought my wife and children to the pool on Sunday, and there was no problem. We all swam between 12 p.m. and 5 p.m. It's a very nice pool!" Mujica added. He is one of 56 migrants currently staying at the airy makeshift shelter, all of them men from Venezuela, Ecuador, Nicaragua, Haiti, and the Dominican Republic, according to a worker.

10. (2023) House Oversight Committee Chairman James Comer issues a memo that includes bank records for Hunter Biden, confirming that the president's son received over $20 million from foreign oligarchs during the "Big Guy's" vice presidency.

Fox News reports the 19-page memo provides screenshots of partially redacted bank records, showing millions of dollars in payments from the Ukrainian energy company Burisma Holdings, Russian oligarch Yelena Baturina, and Kazakhstani oligarch Kenes Rakishev. The memo also confirms that then-Vice President Biden met Baturina, Rakishev, and a Burisma representative at several different dinners.

"Then-Vice President Biden met, in person, for significant periods of time, with those individuals or their representatives," Comer's memo goes on to declare, "Then-Vice President Biden joined approximately 20 phone calls on speakerphone with Hunter Biden's foreign business associates and attended dinners with foreign oligarchs who paid huge sums of money to Hunter Biden. Joe Biden, 'the brand,' was the only product the Biden's sold!"

11. (2022) "My beautiful home, Mar-A-Lago in Palm Beach, Florida, is currently under siege, raided, and occupied by a large group of FBI agents." President Trump makes a statement on the unprecedented FBI raid on his home by agents investigating the handling of classified documents that may have been brought there, CNN reports.

12. (2023) President Donald Trump ignores a court order forbidding him from speaking publicly about his federal election conspiracy case as he reveals his plans to continue posting about it on social media while slamming the judge after she warned him not to intimidate witnesses, obstruct justice or try to muddy his ability to have a fair trial," according to sources close to Trump.

Trump criticized Judge Tanya Chutkan, an Obama appointee, as "highly partisan" and "very biased & unfair" on Truth Social early Monday morning, setting up an early test of the limits that Chutkan has imposed on his (lack of) right to free speech as a criminal defendant under the law.

The former president has insisted it's his First Amendment right to defend himself publicly and has always viewed social media as his most direct way of communicating with his voters, two sources close to Trump told CNN and according to legal arguments made by his lawyer to Chutkan. "He'll share what he feels is necessary and if she (Chutkan) has a problem with it, she will address it," one Trump adviser said, referring to Chutkan.

13. (2023) Records show a Chinese-backed biolab in California was awarded over half a million dollars in US taxpayer cash. The black-market lab - which was raided earlier this year - was found to be making illegal COVID and pregnancy tests and storing disease-ridden mice and hundreds of samples of pathogens, blood, and other dubious chemicals. Public records show that the company linked to the lab received nearly $150,000 from the US government under a Covid-era loan program, receiving two separate loans of $74,912 in April 2020 and February 2021.

14. (2023) FEC records reveal that Black PAC, a Dem dark money Super PAC paid a company $11,254,919 to register voters for Joe Biden's 2020 presidential campaign; this same company is implicated in a Michigan police report over voter registration fraud.

A Michigan police investigation into GBI Strategies LLC was initiated following the observation of a Muskegon, Michigan, clerk who noticed an individual depositing 8,000-10,000 completed voter registration applications at the city office on October 8, 2020.

This same individual returned multiple times over the next few weeks, registering an additional 2,500 voters. Disturbingly, many of those registration forms displayed identical handwriting with fraudulent addresses and falsified phone numbers. Additionally, many signatures did not match those on file with Michigan's Secretary of State.

A subsequent raid by Michigan authorities discovered pre-paid gift cards, firearms equipped with silencers, and disposable burner phones. During the 2020 election season, Democratic election committees collectively channeled more than $4 million directly to GBI Strategies LLC.

15. (2023) "Tuesday is the victory day of the jihad of the people of Afghanistan under the leadership of Islamic Emirate against the United States and its allies." On the second anniversary of Biden's disastrous and tragic US troop withdrawal from Afghanistan, a Taliban Ministry of Labor and Social Affairs official declares August 15 "the day of victory against the United States" and announces a public holiday to mark the 2nd anniversary of the Taliban's return to power in Kabul on August 15, 2021. The Taliban government, the Islamic Emirate, relies on its strict interpretation of Islamic law, or Sharia, to rule the poverty-stricken country.

16. (2022) As Joe Biden attempts to revive the dangerous 2015 Iran nuclear deal things heat up when a negotiator for Tehran dares to seek guarantees that his government, "will be compensated if a future US president pulls out of the pact," CNN reports. Last week European Union officials sent the US and Iran what it called the "final text" of a revived deal to limit Tehran's nuclear program in exchange for sanctions relief. Iran's regional diplomat reports his government has reservations about the possibility of a future president (Trump) pulling out of the new deal, unleashing new sanctions on the country.

Needless to say, President Trump (if elected) would also put a major hurt in Iran's quest for obtaining nukes that would put Israel and the entire free world in great jeopardy. Later, Iran's chief adviser Tweeted that an agreement is "closer than ever."

17. (2023) The Taliban's takeover of Afghanistan proves particularly heartbreaking to American combat vets who fought and sacrificed there. Across 20 years of combat, almost 800,000 troops deployed to the war zone, many more than once. Images of the American withdrawal and questions about the war's legacy potentially trigger the already alarmingly high suicide rate (twenty-two per day) experienced by those courageous soldiers who sacrificed on America's behalf.

18. (2023) A New Jersey court ordered Starbucks to pay an additional $2.7 million to a former employee who sued the company for wrongful termination after she was fired for being White. In June, a jury ruled in favor of Shannon Philips, who worked at Starbucks for 13 years as regional director over the Philadelphia area. The jury returned a verdict of $25.6 million. In an order Wednesday, Judge Joel Slomsky said Starbucks has to make the additional payment for damages.

Phillips was fired after the arrest of two Black men at a Philadelphia Starbucks in April 2018. That incident sparked outrage. Starbucks did not comment on the matter.

19. (2023) Long among the most sensitive subjects inside the West Wing, Hunter Biden's legal saga has reportedly frustrated the "Big Guy" to the point he refuses to talk about him. The probe into Hunter Biden is now 1 of 2 special counsel investigations, the other being an inquiry into his father's handling of classified documents after leaving the Senate and the vice president's office. It's apparent Biden's patented claim to a moral high ground is collapsing beneath him like a massive sinkhole.

20. (1998) Bill Clinton surrendered a DNA sample to Kenneth Starr for comparison with a reported semen stain on the infamous blue dress owned by Monica Lewinsky.

21. (2023) Oliver Anthony's Music's smash hit "Rich Men North of Richmond," an anti-Washington anthem that depicts politicians as depraved and out of touch and wanting "total control" over the lives of the working class, debuts at No. 1 on Billboard's Hot 100 singles chart.

Singer Christopher Anthony Lunsford, unknown just weeks before, bests the likes of Taylor Swift, Morgan Wallen, Olivia Rodrigo, Miley Cyrus, and other A-list performers. Billboard reports it's the first time an artist has launched "atop the list with no prior chart history in any form."

22. (2023) In a 2-1 decision delivered Friday by the DC Circuit federal appeals court it is determined that January 6 protestor, James Little, cannot receive a sentence of prison followed by probation – what is sometimes called a "split sentence" – for his petty offense. "Probation and imprisonment are alternative sentences that cannot generally be combined," the appeals court wrote. Judges in DC's federal trial-level courts had used "split sentences" for low-level January 6 offenders to briefly jail them as punishment for their role in the historic protest on the Capitol and then to keep them on probation and under court supervision through the next election. The ruling jeopardizes the sentences of some January 6 demonstrators who were convicted of misdemeanors for trespassing and sentenced to both jail time and probation.

23. (2023) "Hearing you talk about your house that had a little fire, you 'almost lost your house and your Corvette,' there were children that were incinerated to *ash*, you f***king old man, you vile human being. You're so out of touch with the common man, you don't even know how to speak to them. The only way you think you can establish commonality with them is to lie. The same thing happened to you no matter what the tragedy is.' Your son wasn't killed in action, by the way, your house didn't burn down. Your children weren't burned to death." A video of an incensed, Maui resident displaying his contempt for Joe Biden goes viral following Biden's visit to the island to view the carnage caused by the wildfires two weeks prior.

Biden had stated that he and Dr. Jill Biden can relate to the tragedy, which destroyed Lahina and killed at least 115 people (many of them children) because the first couple once experienced a kitchen fire in one of their homes that could have potentially damaged his classic Corvette.

24. (2023) US mortgage rates surge to their highest level in 21 years. The 30-year fixed-rate mortgage averaged 7.09% in the week ending August 17, up from 6.96% the week before, according to data from Freddie Mac released Thursday.

A year prior, the 30-year fixed-rate was 5.13%. Rates have been above 6.5% since the end of May and climbing higher since mid-July. The last time rates were over 7% was in November of last year when they hit 7.08%. This week's average rate is the highest the 30-year, fixed-rate mortgage has been since April 2002 when it was 7.13%.

As of June 2024, the rate is 7.42%.

25. (2023) Former NBA player Enes Kanter Freedom, blackballed by the NBA for speaking out on the league's cozy relationship with the Communist Chinese government threatens to put on a wig, change his name to "Eneshia and dominate the WNBA promising to average 60 points and 30 rebounds per contest. Fortunately, the highly skilled 7-foot 270-pound center is just making a point later saying, "If I decided to identify myself as a woman and decided to play in the WNBA … would that be fair to all the women who have been chasing their dreams since they were a little kid?"

26. (2021) An ISIS member carries out a suicide attack at the Hamid Karzai International Airport in Kabul airport, killing 13 U.S. service members and at least 170 Afghans during Joe Biden's dreadful troop withdrawal. Among the service members killed are 11 Marines, 1 Army paratrooper, and 1 Navy corpsman. Biden later deems his decision "hard and messy."

27. (2021) The Internet erupted over the report that child actors were used in the first video of a YouTube series with Kamala Harris called "Get Curious with Vice President Harris." The video shows Harris talking to a group of children about her love of science, excitement over being able to see moon craters through a telescope, and the importance of having big dreams.

Following the release of the video, it was revealed that the children auditioned for the series when one child actor told a local news affiliate he had submitted a monologue and was interviewed for his role. The VEEP is mocked for her mannerisms throughout the video, which shows her acting overly animated as she talks with the children. Finally, adding insult to injury, it's discovered a Canadian company produced the video.

28. (2023) Dem CA Attorney General, Rob Banta, files a lawsuit against the Chino Valley Unified School District over its new policy requiring that parents be notified when a child tells a teacher they want to be recognized by a different gender identity or pronoun than the one listed on their birth certificate. Additionally, the School District's policy requires notification if a student requests to use facilities like a different bathroom or participate in "sex-segregated school programs and activities," like a sports team that doesn't align with their sex on official records.

Bonta's suit challenges the policy stating, "The forced outing policy wrongfully endangers the physical, mental, and emotional well-being of non-conforming students who lack an accepting environment in the classroom and at home." Clearly, the School District's audacity in suggesting parents have any rights in issues pertaining to their children's welfare strikes a nerve with CA bureaucrats.

29. (2023) President Donald Trump's campaign reports it has raised $7.1 million since the former president was processed at an Atlanta jail last week in the Georgia election subversion case. Trump's fundraising total for the past three weeks, following his indictment and arraignment in Washington related to the federal January 6 case and then his surrender and processing at the Fulton County jail in Georgia, is reportedly close to $20 million with his highest grossing day occurring on Friday, the day following his arrest in Georgia when at he raised $4.18 million, sources state.

30. (2023) The Daily News reports ICE officials are sounding the alarm over a new Biden admin proposal to outsource key immigration enforcement responsibilities and services, which they say could allow the administration to fund activist groups. Biden's new "Release and Reporting Management" (RRM) program is reportedly intended to boost the administration's efforts to limit immigration enforcement and expand social services by handing out lucrative contracts to activist groups.

31. (2023) NY Post reports the FBI is scrambling to find more than a dozen Uzbek nationals who were brought into the US by a smuggler with ties to ISIS. The worry is that the FBI is currently spread too thin to look into the allegation as the Bureau's manpower is focused on investigating "domestic terrorists" like angry parents attending school board meetings and being mean to board members.

SEPTEMBER

1. (2015) "Poor people have been voting for Democrats for 50 years and they're still poor." Sir Charles Barkley

2. (2022) An Iraq War veteran and former Democratic Party official criticized the presence of US Marines in the backdrop of Joe Biden's speech in Philadelphia, during which he issued stinging political criticism of Republicans. "We need to make sure that our military is as removed from politics as possible and it's not right if a Democrat uses the military as a political pawn and it's not right if the Republican Party does it as well. None of our politicians or elected leaders should do that," Allison Jaslow, a former executive director of the Democratic Congressional Campaign Committee, tells CNN's Brianna Keilar on "New Day."

In Biden's defense, he has already weaponized the DOJ and undoubtedly assumed it wouldn't be an issue to flaunt the military in the same manner other third-world thug dictators do.

3. (2023) A study by John Lott (Crime Research.org) finds concealed carry laws may reduce murder rates in the long run. The study, which was published in the journal Economic Inquiry, found that "the effect of concealed carry laws on murder rates takes time to manifest but that it is *negative* and statistically significant in the following years. In this context the word "negative," means concealed carry is reducing the murder rate."

The study was conducted using a sample of all 50 states from 1970 to 2018. The researchers controlled for a variety of factors that could affect murder rates, such as the unemployment rate, the poverty rate, and the incarceration rate. The researchers found that the effect of concealed carry laws on murder rates is heterogeneous, meaning the effect of these laws may vary depending on the state or the type of law.

For example, the study found that Constitutional Carry laws, which allow people to carry guns without a permit, may have a larger effect on murder rates than right-to-carry laws, which require people to obtain a permit in order to carry guns.

The news study's findings are important because they suggest that concealed carry laws, and in particular constitutional carry, may be an effective way to reduce murder rates. As expected, anti-gun researchers immediately lambaste the study noting there is no room for factual data in the debate.

4. (2023) "They believe race is first and foremost the thing you should always see everywhere, which I find interesting because that used to be the position of the Ku Klux Klan." Bill Maher compares Woke liberals to the malevolent White supremacist hate group.

5. (2023) "I have no home to go to." Doddering Joe Biden makes a statement to reporters in Rehoboth Beach, Delaware following a mass service. He declares his recent string of stays at his Rehoboth Beach house are not vacations since he can't return to his Wilmington home while it is undergoing security upgrades.

Biden's comments cause a reporter to ask if he is suggesting that he's "homeless?" Biden responds, "I can tell you all about being homeless, man. I was homeless for 10 years. My Dad said, "Joey, I am going to teach you about being homeless. I was 3 years old, and he threw me out in the snow. All I had was a dog biscuit. And you know what? I was happy to have that dog biscuit. I mean I was 3. I can tell you all about being homeless, man!"

(Okay, maybe Joe didn't say that last part).

6. (2023) Deranged View co-host, Joy Behar, reports former President Donald Trump was at fault for the torrential rains that flooded out the Burning Man festival. More than 70,000 people were forced to shelter in place in Nevada's Black Rock Desert on Friday night after hours of rainfall created flash flooding on the grounds of the remote weeklong festival. "This is one of the many tragedies this summer due to climate change. This is the one… the number one existential problem now," Behar informs her captive zombie audience.

7. (2016) Barack Obama goes all in on the side of Colin Kaepernick's protest stating, "He's exercising his constitutional right to make a statement. I think there is a long history of sports figures doing so. I think there are a lot of ways you can do it when it comes to the flag and national anthem." The "bromance" between Barack and Kap is clearly forged in their mutual contempt for America.

8. (2023) Residents in the New York area represented by AOC blast her for sharing a video last month that said propaganda was being fed to the American public about inflation. The video, from left-wing New Zealand group Aotearoa Liberation League, blamed "greedy shareholders" for creating "propaganda" about inflation. "The price of everything keeps going up; meanwhile, the corporations selling those things are making massive profits," the video states. "The goal of the capitalist is to disconnect these two facts from one another. So they use this concept of inflation."

"The propaganda around inflation and cost of living is so powerful that we forget the very basic fact that corporations set the prices for their products," the video continued. "If a corporation raises its prices and then makes record profits, that's not some invisible monster. It's just a bunch of greedy shareholders." AOC's constituents in the 14th district are reportedly livid at her and question whether she is simply dishonest or actually stupid enough to believe her own statements. Smart money rides on the latter.

9. (2008) "I'm told Chuck Graham, state senator is here. Stand up, Chuck, let 'em see you. Oh, God love you. What am I talking about? I'll tell you what, you're making everybody else stand up, though pal." Joe Biden telling Missouri state senator Chuck Graham to stand at a campaign rally before realizing that Graham is in a wheelchair.

10. (2023) "These men knew what they were doing. I have NO DOUBT they have done this before. Yet they are still on OUR STREETS. Killing mothers. Giving babies psychological trauma that a lifetime of therapy cannot ease. With no hesitation and no remorse. And: "REMEMBER ME when you are thinking about supporting letting juveniles and young people out of custody to roam our streets instead of HOLDING THEM ACCOUNTABLE FOR THEIR ACTIONS." NY Rep Shivanthi Sathanandan - an ultra-strong advocate for defunding and dismantling the Minnesota Police Department for "systematically failing the Black Community" changes her tune after her face is beaten and bloodied during a carjacking that occurred in broad daylight, in front of her own home and her children.

The incident gives credence to Irving Kristol's quip, "A conservative is a liberal who's been mugged."

11. (2023) MSNBC writer, Ja'han Jones, blasts NYC Mayor Eric Adams after Adams' delivers a speech raising concerns about the migrant crisis

spilling over into the Big Apple. Ja'han calls the Mayor out for "bigoted thinking inspired by the right" before inadvertently paying Adams a huge compliment by dubbing him "Black Trump."

12. (2023) Two retired generals, and a retired colonel, all three graduates of the U.S. Military Academy (USMA) at West Point, sign a statement, nominally representing the long list of West Point graduates known as the "Long Gray Line," accusing the academy of violating its core values and imposing socialist, anti-American indoctrination.

When you wonder why so many of our military commanders are involved in scandals, and accused of moral and ethical lapses, and even crimes, look no further than West Point, and the other national military academies.

In their August 17 missive emailed to a long email list and posted on the website of the MacArthur Society of West Point graduates' senior officers, LTG Thomas McInerney, USAF (Ret), MG Paul E. Vallely, US Army (Ret), and Col Andrew O'Meara, US Army (Ret), argue that the academy no longer truly enforces the proud institution's Cadet Honor Code.

Despite West Point's motto being "Duty, Honor, Country," and that motto forming the basis of the Cadet Honor Code, it is now enforced less than half the time.

Rather than resulting in expulsion as in the past, the officers note that "today, the Academy's website makes the casual web disclaimer that over 50% of convicted violators of the honor code are excused and allowed to graduate."

But even more alarming than just letting unethical cadets graduate to form the backbone of the Army's officer corps, cadets are increasingly being indoctrinated in neo-Marxist socialist ideology "that runs counter to the noble principles of the Constitution."

They add: "The corruption of cadet instruction with socialist doctrine is further demonstrated by a pronounced bias in selecting guest speakers who have been almost exclusively liberal."

13. (2023) Former President Trump calls on Republicans to invoke the 25th Amendment, which involves presidential succession in the case the president cannot carry out the powers and duties of the office, against Joe Biden as a

consequence of his new prisoner swap deal with Iran, which Trump states proves Biden's utter "incompetence." Additionally, Biden's deal releases $6 billion in frozen Iranian funds to the government. The good news is that the evil, maniacal terrorist regime "promises" it will not use the windfall "to promote terrorism." Biden stands by his decision reportedly claiming if you can't trust a terrorist, who can you trust?

14. (2019) During the third Democratic debate Beto O'Rourke reiterated his support for a mandatory gun-buyback program and proclaimed, "Hell yes, we're going to take your AR 15, your AK47." Beto claims the buy-back of assault-style rifles is part of his plan to curb gun violence and the rise of white nationalism.

15. (2023) Rob Reiner laments, "Since the Civil War the threat to American Democracy has not been greater than it is today! The only way that democracy can go forward is if former President Donald Trump goes to prison." Democracy responds immediately stating, "Archie Bunker was right, Rob Reiner is a "Meathead" (dead from the neck up) and his opinions are only relevant to his 2.2 million followers of equally vacuous Meatheads!

16. (2020) Axios reports that "The arson, vandalism, and looting during the left-wing media-ascribed "mostly peaceful" protests following the death of George Floyd will result in at least $1 billion to $2 billion of paid insurance claims."

The $1 billion-plus riot damage is the most expensive in insurance history. Not only was there an irreplaceable human toll (as dozens of people were killed or injured in the violent unrest), but thousands of businesses and properties—many minority-owned— were looted, torched, or otherwise vandalized new reporting from Axios reveals. Additionally, there are many reasons why this figure vastly underestimates the true damage wrought by the looting and violence including the fact that the Axios report only measures insured losses, the obvious problem being not all the damages were insured. Aside from the startling evidence, the protests continue to be labeled "mostly peaceful."

17. (2023) After previously slamming inquiries into her pornographic website as "gutter politics" Dem Virginia state Senate candidate Susanna Gibson, who claimed she was raising money for a "good cause" by performing wild sex acts online, could be charged with prostitution.

Earlier this week, the Washington Post reported that Gibson, 40, hosted raunchy live webcam shows on OnlyFans competitor Chaturbate, after announcing her candidacy in the race to represent Virginia's District 57 in July 2022.

Gibson's account, "HotWifeExperience," saw her soliciting viewers to pay her in the platform's tokens to watch her urinate on camera or be choked out by her husband, lawyer David Gibson. "Y'all can watch me pee if you tip me some tokens," she said according to the Daily Wire. "Again, I'm raising money for a good cause."

According to Virginia law, the Democrat may have violated the state's prostitution law by performing the acts on camera for money, which is a Class 1 misdemeanor.

18. (2020) Conservatives take to Twitter to blast the residents of Martha's Vineyard for promptly removing the 50 illegal immigrants that Florida Gov. Ron DeSantis sent to the island last week. Fox News Digital reports DeSantis sent two planes carrying 50 illegal immigrants to the ritzy elite summer vacation spot in an attempt to highlight the record influx of illegal immigrants at the southern border, which has overwhelmed many border towns and exhausted their resources.

Martha's Vineyard activated the National Guard in response and released a statement calling the situation a "humanitarian crisis." The 50 migrants were ultimately loaded onto buses two days after arriving and transported off Martha's Vineyard to military housing on the Cape Cod mainland.

19. (2023) New records reveal that Dr. Anthony Fauci and his wife Christine had a total net worth of over $11 million at the time Fauci left his government post last year. According to Fox News, the termination papers for the former director of the National Institute of Allergy and Infectious Diseases show that the Faucis' net worth was up by $2 million since before the Chinese Coronavirus pandemic, despite dipping slightly between 2021 and 2022.

"During the pandemic years, the Fauci's became deca-millionaires with their household net worth exceeding $10 million. Last year was a tough year in the markets, however, Fauci's net worth was still up sharply from $7.6 million in 2019," said Adam Andrzejewski, CEO of the watchdog group OpenTheBooks.

20. (2020) In about as awkward a moment as imaginable, "Blackish" actor, Anthony Anderson, forces Jimmy Kimmel to recite the mantra "Black Lives Matter" during the Emmys. The lack of commitment in Kimmel's voice is plainly unacceptable to Anderson who orders an uncomfortable Kimmel to repeat the phrase several times.

21. (2021) Yet another image of Canadian Prime Minister Justin Trudeau in blackface at the 2001 Arabian Nights party - this time in color - emerges just in time for the Canadian Federal Election. The photo, released on Sunday by Canadian Proud, shows the liberal icon in a turban and robe, with his tongue sticking out. The world leader has also covered his face with dark makeup. The latest insensitive image of the Canadian Prime Minister, who has a checkered history of blackface, has been slammed as a national embarrassment and Trudeau branded a 'clown' by many online.

22. (2023) While interviewing Gen Mark Milley, CNN's Fareed Zakaria, asks, "Is the U.S. military too woke?" Milley squirms momentarily before replying, "No, not at all. You know, I'm not even sure what that word truly means. This military is a lot of things, but woke it is not. So, I take exception to that. I think that people say those things for reasons that are their own reasons. But it's not true. It's not accurate. And it is not to say, by the way, that there are not some things out there that could be fit into that category. But I don't think it certainly is, it is not a broad-brush description of the U.S. military as it exists today."

Milley's words ring hollow, however, as evidence that he has fully supported the woke affliction on the military is documented. In June 2021, testifying before the House Armed Services Committee on Joe Biden's 2022 budget request, Milley defended the reading of Critical Race Theory texts by the US military, asserting, "I've read Mao Tse-Tung, I've read Karl Marx, I've read Lenin and I personally found it offensive that we are accusing our general officers, our commissioned, non-commissioned officers, of being 'woke' because we're studying some theories that are out there."

Yes, General Milley, the "theories" of Mao, Marx, and Lenin are definitely not woke and is something our military should be devoting its time to studying.

Milley goes on to advocate for troops being educated on "white rage," saying, "I do think it's important actually for those of us in uniform to be open-minded and be widely read and the United States Military Academy is a university, and it is important that we train, and we understand, and I want to understand white rage and I'm white."

The NY Post reported in September 2022 that Air Force cadets had been instructed not to use gender-specific terms like "Mom" or "Dad" and to replace such terms with words such as "parent" or "caregiver." That instruction was featured at the Air Force Academy in Colorado as part of cadets' "Diversity and Inclusion (D&I) training." "Our leaders have deemed D&I a warfighting imperative," the cadets were reportedly told.

23. (2019) "My message is that we'll be watching you! This is all wrong. I shouldn't be up here. I should be back in school on the other side of the ocean. Yet you all come to us young people for hope. How dare you? You have stolen my dreams and my childhood with your empty words. And yet I'm one of the lucky ones. People are suffering. People are dying. Entire ecosystems are collapsing. We are in the beginning of a mass extinction, and all you can talk about is money and fairy tales of eternal economic growth. How dare you!" Petulant child and climate activist Greta Thunberg, 16, addresses the U.N.'s Climate Action Summit in New York City.

24. (2023) "By the way that boy, that man's got biceps bigger than my thighs!" Joe Biden, once again, refers to a black person in what people in his own party consider to be a derogatory manner, this time referring to rapper LL Cool J as "boy" after he had just butchered his name by introducing him as "LL Jay Cool J, uh!" This incident is made even more special, as Biden's speech was before the Congressional Black Caucus!

25. (2023) Joe Biden announces plans to possibly ban guns under a national emergency declaration. The Washington Post reports Biden's new "Office of Gun Violence Prevention" will declare "a national gun violence health public emergency" as part of a plan by Biden to go around Congress and impose anti-gun measures through Executive Orders.

The Post reports the anti-gun office will be run by a "high-profile activist from the Community Justice Action Fund," a notorious "Defund The Police" organization that supports gun confiscation and funneling billions of tax dollars to political activists to work as "violence interrupters."

26. (2022) A seminar on transgender visibility is held at the US Air Force Academy according to a new report by the Washington Free Beacon.

The report, depicting an invitation emailed to all cadets at the academy, reveals that attendees spent an hour discussing "Transgender Visibility" in the Air Force. Karin DeAngelis and Joseph Cumin, members of the academy's faculty, held two presentations as part of the event. Sec of Defense Lloyd Austin has appointed each member of the new advisory committee, according to the press release. The Air Force's gender-inclusive training reportedly informs cadets they are no longer allowed to use the words "mom" and "dad. Once again, taxpayer money is well spent!

27. (2023) Calling her "a key leader in the Biden-Harris Administration's effort to end our nation's gun violence epidemic," Joe Biden taps Kamala Harris to oversee the first-ever "White House Office of Gun Violence Prevention."

"The new Office of Gun Violence Prevention will play a critical role in implementing President Biden's and my efforts to reduce violence to the fullest extent under the law," Harris said in the White House statement. VP Harris has proved to be the go-to person in the administration and will now be able to add "Gun Confiscation Czar" to her growing list of Czar failures.

28. (2023) New video shows hundreds of migrants cheering and waving Venezuelan flags atop a US-bound cargo train, a continuation of scenes over the weekend when more than 5,000 were seen boarding another freighter to get into the US. The clip shows a slightly smaller procession of several hundred migrants standing on a stopped train near Eagle Pass, TX a border town whose mayor says it has reached the "breaking point" due to accepting more than 2,000 per day.

29. (2023) "This is highway f–king robbery!" Miami Heat's star forward Jimmy Butler gets a case of sticker shock when he fills up his exotic car at a California gas station. Butler complained while he pumped premium into his $3.6 million Bugatti Chiron Pur Sport at a gas station in Los Angeles.

Still sweaty from a workout, the 34-year-old NBA All-Star stared at the price on the pump in astonishment as the camera zoomed in on the digital display at Jack Colker's Union 76 Gas Station in Beverly Hills, to reveal that the hoops star's ride cost him $145 for just less than 20 gallons of gas.

According to Fox News, the cost of regular gas in Southern California is almost $7 dollars a gallon, while premium, which is what Butler likely put in his sports car, hit $7.19. Jimmy Butler reportedly makes $37.6 million dollars a year.

Think of the hardships endured by CA residents who are barely able to make ends meet due to inflation, gasoline prices, and "Bidenomics." "Can y'all believe it costs $145 to fill up a Bugatti? This is crazy! ... Unheard of," Butler fumed as he drove away from the scene of the robbery. Thankfully there is no way for Jimmy Buckets to foresee that the CA Air Resources Board will increase the gas tax by yet another 52 cents by the year 2026.

30. (2023) A former Indian diplomat claims that there is a "credible rumor" that Canadian Prime Minister Justin Trudeau's plane at the recent G20 meeting was "full of cocaine." Deepak Vohra, who was a former Indian ambassador to Sudan, made the claim on Monday on Indian television, also saying that the Canadian leader "has definitely gone insane."

"When Justin Trudeau came to India for the G20 this month, his plane was full of cocaine," Vohra said during a show on Zee News, according to the Toronto Sun, "He did not come out of his room for two days," Vohra claimed that police dogs had discovered cocaine on Trudeau's plane during the G20 summit earlier in the month.

"My wife saw him at the Delhi airport and said that Trudeau looked depressed and stressed," Vohra continued. "We don't know the reason. I don't know the reality, but social media and some credible rumors suggest that his plane was full of cocaine. He has become lonely. He is now trying to show that he is a Canadian Rambo, and nothing can go wrong in his presence. India has done the right thing by suspending visa services in Canada."

OCTOBER

1. (2020) "With this cruel decision, America has abandoned its leadership role in providing safety to refugees who are most in need of resettlement. The Administration's actions are a shameful betrayal of our longstanding bipartisan tradition of generosity and strength and accomplish nothing except failing to protect innocent victims of persecution who pose no threat to our security and have turned to America for safety."

Democrat Senators Dick Durbin and Dianne Feinstein denounce the Trump administration's informing Congress it intends to accept only 15,000 refugees in 2020, a new historic low for the US.

The State Department claims that the "President's proposal for refugee resettlement in Fiscal Year 2021 reflects the Admin's continuing commitment to prioritize the safety and well-being of Americans, especially in light of the ongoing COVID-19 pandemic."

Durbin and Di-Fi are reportedly annoyed that "the safety and well-being of American citizens" have suddenly become a consideration.

2. (2020) Disney announces it will be slapping racism warnings on a number of decades-old movies as they are released on its streaming service Disney+. Subscribers who log on to watch classic films like "Lady and the Tramp" or "Peter Pan" now see stronger advisory messages warning of racist content.

"As part of our ongoing commitment to diversity and inclusion, we are in the process of reviewing our library and adding advisories to content that includes negative depictions or mistreatment of people or cultures," Disney said in an online statement.

"Rather than removing this content, we see an opportunity to spark conversation and open dialogue on history that affects us all," it added. The 1955 animated comedy "Lady and the Tramp" carries an advisory because of its depiction of Siamese cats in a way that perpetuates anti-Asian stereotypes. Disney says the advisory is not new, but it has now been updated and strengthened for this and other films.

Last year, CNN reported that Disney had issued a warning on some movies, such as "Dumbo," that they featured "outdated cultural depictions."

At that time, the description of these films in the streaming service's menu included a warning that "this program is presented as originally created. It may contain outdated cultural depictions." Now, once viewers press play, they see the following message, which cannot be fast-forwarded: "This program includes negative depictions and/or mistreatment of people or cultures. These stereotypes were then and are wrong now. Rather than remove this content, we want to acknowledge its harmful impact, learn from it, and spark conversation to create a more inclusive future together."

A spokesman for Disney reports, "Disney is committed to creating stories with inspirational and aspirational themes that reflect the rich diversity of the human experience around the globe." Walt (RIP) could never have imagined that one day the beloved children's classics he created would be deemed so offensive.

3. (2023) A biographer reveals that former FTX CEO Sam Bankman-Fried wanted to pay former President Donald Trump $5 billion to not pursue reelection. Michael Lewis, the disgraced crypto boss' biographer told "60 Minutes" about the ploy while promoting his upcoming book, "Going Infinite: The Rise and Fall of a New Tycoon."

Interviewer Jon Wertheim said that the admission was "one of the most shocking passages" in Lewis's novel. He said that the Dem donor, who allegedly stole $100 million in FTX deposits to bankroll liberal candidates prior to the 2022-midterm elections, found out that it would take $5 billion for Trump to stop pursuing the White House in 2024. According to Lewis, Bankman-Fried wasn't able to follow through with the offer, as "they were still having these conversations when FTX blew up."

4. (2023) The U.S. Supreme Court denies Liberty Counsel's petition for writ of certiorari regarding a request to review a ruling by the Ninth Circuit Court of Appeals against Sandra Merritt in Planned Parenthood's multimillion-dollar civil lawsuit for her undercover investigation of the abortion giant. The High Court's denial of review was without any comment. The implications of this civil case have far-reaching First Amendment consequences involving free speech and undercover journalism.

Merritt and David Daleiden, founders of the Center for Medical Progress, released videos in 2015 following a 30-month undercover investigation exposing Planned Parenthood and other organ procurement companies regarding aborted baby body parts. Sinister videos show Planned Parenthood executives haggling over prices of aborted baby body parts and discussing ways they can change abortion procedures to obtain more intact organs.

5. (2023) Newsweek reports the FBI has decided to classify supporters of former President Donald Trump as potential "domestic extremists." The report goes on to state the FBI's targeting of Trump supporters "drastically increased under Joe Biden and that "nearly two-thirds of the FBI's current investigations" target Trump supporters who are being (falsely) accused of violating what the bureau calls "anti-riot" laws.

Newsweek published national security reporter William M. Arkin's 4,300-word report amid growing concerns and criticism from conservatives and independents about the scope of the FBI's actions and its apparent weaponization under Biden over the past few years.

Days before Newsweek published a report on the FBI's targeting of Trump supporters, Heritage Foundation President Kevin Roberts, stated his belief that the FBI is well past the point of reform and "needs to be started over from scratch and rebuilt," adding, "This is not a law enforcement agency. It's a political weapon."

Following the riot at the Capitol on Jan. 6, 2021, which occurred two weeks before Biden took over from Trump, the FBI reformed one of its classifications of extremists to include Americans who support conservative or libertarian political organizations and individuals, Newsweek reported. The FBI calls that classification "anti-government or anti-authority violent extremists-other," or AGAAVE.

National Security reporter Arkin cited government insiders who told him that FBI officials regularly use the terms "MAGA" and "Trump supporters" to describe those who fit the AGAAVE profile. Arkin quoted a senior intelligence official as telling him: "Trump's army constitutes the greatest threat of violence domestically, that's the reality and the problem set."

Although the FBI told Newsweek in an official statement that the bureau does not target Americans based on political belief, its previous actions and similar ones by its parent agency, the Justice Department, and top elected Democrats indicate otherwise. In 2021 and 2022, the DOJ labeled dozens of conservative parents as "domestic terrorists" subject to FBI investigation because they raised concerns at local school board meetings. In recent months, the FBI also has reportedly targeted pro-life activists.

Biden repeatedly has labeled citizens "MAGA" Republicans a "threat not only to his policy proposals but to the very soul of this country!" Ironically, Biden fails to recognize the horrific impact his own soullessness is having on the nation.

6. (2023) In a CNN interview, Hillary Clinton proclaims her hatred for President Trump, his supporters, and (apparently) "freedom of speech," floating the idea of "formally deprogramming" Trump supporters and his "cult" wing of devotees.

Hillary closed with her trademark cackle, seemingly oblivious to the fact that many Americans are repulsed by the sight and sound of her.

7. (2023) Evidence released by House Oversight and Accountability Committee Chairman James Comer raises questions about whether Joe Biden was trying to pre-emptively deflect attention from his own problems with retaining government documents when he unleashed the FBI on President Trump for claims of identical issues at Mar-a-Lago in Spring of 2022.

An unidentified source claimed Biden could be heard storming throughout the White House screaming, "C'mon man! Everybody knows there are two tiers of the criminal justice system under my administration!"

8. (2023) Harvard student groups draw intense campus and national backlash for signing onto a statement that they "hold the Israeli regime entirely responsible for all unfolding violence" in the wake of the invasion of Israel by the Islamist terrorist group Hamas.

Authored by the Harvard Undergraduate Palestine Solidarity Committee and originally co-signed by 33 other Harvard student organizations Saturday, the statement came under fire from federal lawmakers, University professors, and other students. The statement was initially released on the PSC's Instagram page.

"Today's events did not occur in a vacuum," the statement reads. "For the last two decades, millions of Palestinians in Gaza have been forced to live in an open-air prison. Israeli officials promise to 'open the gates of hell,' and the massacres in Gaza have already commenced."

"In the coming days, Palestinians will be forced to bear the full brunt of Israel's violence. The apartheid regime is the only one to blame," it continues. Parents of Harvard students admit they have concluded they'd be prouder if their kids were prison inmates than Harvard undergraduates.

9. (2023) "BLM Grassroots," releases a statement in support of the Palestinian people that likens Palestinian terrorism to BLM's own activism. BLM Chicago shares a "celebratory" graphic of a paraglider with a Palestinian flag pointing out of his parachute and praises the evil terrorists who paraglided into an Israeli music festival to viciously murder 260 innocent attendees. As has been the case in most major US cities, pro-Palestinian protestors gathered Monday on the streets of Chicago to cheer on the Palestinian cause, which in this latest bout of terrorism has resulted in 1,400 deaths of innocents including the beheading of 40 babies.

BLM Chicago is just one of the many BLM branches around the country that have publicly backed Palestinian fighters following the murderous rampage Hamas unleashed on innocent Israeli civilians. The Greatest Generation's tears fall like rain.

10. (2023) Squad associate Rep. Rashida Tlaib is slammed for continuing to display a Palestinian flag outside her Capitol office after the mass slaughter of innocent Israelis by Hamas terrorists days earlier. GOP Rep. Max Miller of Ohio is among those replying to the abomination and he reveals he has introduced an amendment that would ban foreign flags from Congress. "The Palestinian flag should not have a place here. Instead, "the halls of Congress belong to America" and "should be reserved for flags that embody our great nation," he wrote on X.

Tlaib blasts Israel's "occupation" policies and advocates for "dismantling the apartheid system that creates the suffocating, dehumanizing conditions that can lead to resistance" but fails to condemn Hamas for its heinous slaughter of at least 1,400 innocent civilian men, women, children and babies during the unprovoked attack.

11. (2023) BabylonBee reports that, in a tragic development, the Pride flag displayed outside Representative Tlaib's office in the Capitol was tossed off of a roof by the Palestinian flag she had been keeping adjacent to it. "We are

deeply saddened that the Palestinian flag, who [sic] we thought just wanted peace and autonomy, suddenly yeeted [sic] the Pride flag off the roof," said Ms. Tlaib in a statement. "We of course are saddened by the tragic attack on the LGBTQ community, but equally saddened by the oppression that forced the peace-loving Palestine flag to commit this terrible act. At the end of the day, we blame the Jews."

As the Capitol Police secured the area, agents expressed sorrow that the calamity was entirely preventable. "We should have seen it coming," said Officer Dan Rawls, as he surveyed the flag's remains. "Those two flags, they just never seem to mix well. Someone always winds up thrown off a building."

12. (2023) The DHS admits in a September report that foreign terrorists are exploiting the Biden-manufactured border crisis to illegally enter the United States. The 2024 "Homeland Threat Assessment," released last month by the DHS Office of Intelligence and Analysis includes an admission by the agency that international terrorists are looking to capitalize on the Biden admin's open border policies and the resulting influx of illegal immigration across the U.S.-Mexico border to enter the American homeland. Under the section titled, "Border and Immigration Security," the agency acknowledges that "individuals with potential terrorism connections" are actively attempting to enter the U.S. courtesy of the Biden-created border crisis.

The Homeland Security Committee Republican reports that since Joe Biden took office, there have been 7.5 million encounters nationwide and 6.2 million encounters at the Southwest border, in addition to 1.7 million "known" gotaways." Additionally, the New York Post points out that number doesn't even include the potentially millions of other "gotaways" who evaded capture by CBP agents.

To date in Fiscal Year 2023, 169 individuals whose names appear on the terror watchlist were stopped trying to cross the U.S.-Mexico border between ports of entry. 18 were apprehended in September alone.

In FY2023 CBP has arrested 35,433 aliens with criminal convictions or outstanding warrants nationwide, including 598 known gang members, 178 of those being MS-13 members.

In FY2023 CBP has seized 27,293 pounds of fentanyl coming across the Southwest border—enough to kill more than 6 billion people.

In its most recent threat assessment, DHS specifically highlighted Iran and its "intent to plot attacks against current and former US government officials." The assessment reports that "Iran relies on individuals with pre-existing access to the United States for surveillance and lethal plotting, using dual nationals, members of criminal networks, and private investigators," the report reads, adding that Tehran has even attempted to carry out plots "that do not require international travel for operatives." The report also listed Hezbollah, another Iranian-backed terrorist group operating out of Lebanon, as another source of potential foreign terror threats.

The revelations present even more staggering evidence of the abject failure of Joe Biden in executing his number one duty – keeping American citizens safe.

13. (2023) In an Op-Ed for The Hill, liberal commentator Juan Williams shockingly refers to Joe Biden as "our third Black president." The United States has had only one African-American president, though Toni Morrison famously called Bill Clinton "the first Black president." Williams notes that "by Morrison's standard, President Joe Biden is our nation's third Black president," defending his asinine statement by citing Biden's naming of Kamala Harris as his running mate, the appointment of Supreme Court Justice Ketanji Brown Jackson, and naming Lloyd Austin as the first ever African American Secretary of Defense. According to recent polls, however, someone forgot to remind Black Americans of Biden's achievements on their behalf as record numbers are backing President Trump in 2024 due to the fact that he was the only President who ever actually cared enough about them to enact policies that improved their lives.

14. (2023) The Starbucks Workers United Union posts "Solidarity with Palestine" on social media platform X above an image of a bulldozer operated by Hamas tearing down a fence in the Gaza strip in the aftermath of the slaughter, torture rape, and abductions of innocent Israelis days earlier. The union's account deletes the tweet, but not before it sparks calls for a boycott of Starbucks on social media. Starbucks Workers United reportedly declined to respond to CNN's request for comment.

15. (2023) The advocacy group Climate Power announces it is committing $80 million in advertising to praise Joe Biden's climate and environment agenda ahead of the 2024 election. The ad campaign reportedly aims to

inform voters about the president's wide-ranging climate and clean energy agenda.

Lori Lodes, executive director of Climate Power states, "People overwhelmingly support what President Biden has done to combat climate change but only if they hear about it. Our campaign plans to bridge the information gap around the clean energy plan by meeting Americans where they are and telling the story of our climate progress."

The Biden administration has also received praise from the youth-led climate group the Sunrise Movement after moving to create the first-ever American Climate Corps. Meanwhile, Conservatives laugh at the plan stating you can put $80 million worth of lipstick on a pig, but it will still be Joe Biden.

16. (2023) During an interview, Naftali Bennett, a former Israeli prime minister, criticizes Anderson Cooper for the way CNN (and the media as a whole) covered the Gaza hospital explosion that occurred earlier in the week. The hospital was bombed by Israel, according to a fabrication made by the Hamas-run Palestinian Ministry of Health. Before senior officials from Israel, the United States, and Europe presented evidence that categorically rejected those assertions, the media hastily embraced that narrative. More than 500 people are believed to have died in the explosion, which was brought on by a missile fired by Palestinian militants.

"There are no two sides to this hospital. Either it was bombed by Israel, or it was targeted by someone else on the Palestinian side. If two people come and say, one says it's raining outside and the other said it's dry, you don't bring the quotes of both sides. You just g**d**n open the window and look whether it's raining or not. That's what we did," Bennett said.

"And this hospital, in fact, it's a parking lot, was hit definitely a hundred percent by an Islamic jihad barrage shot fired at 6:59 p.m. We have three different videos from different angles showing it. We have the ballistics. We know that an Israeli bomb would have created a crater, which does not exist. We know that the propellant in the rocket, because it was a long-term rocket targeted for Israel, so a lot of that propellant was still in the rocket, which created a lot of fire. We have two Hamas terrorists talking to each other and saying and admitting that it is from Islamic jihad," Bennett schooled a bewildered Anderson Cooper.

17. (2023) "I did the mug shot in Atlanta. I don't think I've ever made so much money in my life (as) that mug shot." President Trump celebrates with his supporters in West Palm Beach following the bonanza his fundraising campaign has experienced from sales of posters, T-shirts, coffee cups, and other merchandise that feature his glowering mug shot with the tag line, "NEVER SURRENDER!" An astounding $24.5 million has reportedly poured into the President's main campaign account from July to September and the haul marks a surge from the $17.7 million his campaign took in during the previous quarter when he was indicted in NY on clearly contrived charges related to the ludicrous Stormy Daniels payoff scandal charges. A CNN analysis of the newly filed reports underscores how his campaign has turned his court appearances into a "financial bonanza" a fact that seemingly escapes his corrupt political antagonists.

18. (2023) CNN anchor Erin Burnett raves over Hamas terrorists' treatment of civilian hostages following the release of two elderly Jewish women whom they'd held captive stating, "Yes, it was remarkable. And she (hostage) did have criticism for the IDF. And you know how they (IDF), obviously, weren't there. Also, Poppy, some things stand out in their mundane necessity. You are talking about tunnels. We know these tunnels have ventilation. We know that they've been known to have air-conditioning. This is what we have heard from the Israelis over the years. But the fact that she is saying she was held underground for more than two weeks, that there was shampoo, there were antibiotics, there was a guard per hostage in the experience she had, that there were medics and paramedics. And, obviously, she is elderly. The other woman who was released, was also elderly and had medical needs, and they had the medicine needed, and if not something similar to replace it, it is pretty stunning, because you've got to contrast that with what's happening above the ground, right, where there isn't water, never mind shampoo, OK. They don't have water. They're using toilet water. There is no morphine for any kind of amputations, antibiotics, no, right. But Hamas had stockpiled all of that and has all of that underground, and that's what we are learning from her." Unsubstantiated sources report Burnett is later overheard saying she envies the hostages and wishes she too, could enjoy the pampering they are receiving courtesy of Hamas terrorists.

19. (2023) "Today we welcomed nearly 300 Americans who have been in Israel since last week when the violent attacks by Hamas terrorists began." Governor Ron DeSantis celebrates the safe return of nearly 300 Americans, (including 91 children) stranded in war-torn Israel after he authorized the

Florida Department of Emergency Management to carry out "logistical, rescue and evacuation operations" for Florida residents trapped in Israel.

20. (2020) USA Today reports that VP Joe Biden leveraged $1 billion in aid to "persuade" Ukraine to oust its top prosecutor, Viktor Shokin in March 2016 because Shokin was investigating Burisma Holdings, the largest gas company in the fledgling democracy, which "coincidentally" boasted Hunter Biden as a highly regarded board member. When asked about his controversial termination Shokin later told Fox News, "They (Biden's) were being bribed. The fact that Joe Biden gave away $1 billion in U.S. money in exchange for my dismissal, my firing, isn't that alone a case of corruption?"

21. (2023) Asked about Biden's "level of concern right now about a potential rise in anti-Semitism," Karine Jean-Pierre immediately pivots and suggests reporters focus on Islamophobia, noting that "Muslims and those perceived to be Muslim have endured a disproportionate number of hate-fueled attacks." Meanwhile, the Anti-Defamation League reports a 388% rise in anti-Semitic incidents over the past two weeks. Americans issue a collective gasp at KJP's tone-deaf and disgusting remark.

22. (2023) American Liberty reports Kingsway Regional School District (Kingsway, New Jersey) has been socially transitioning students behind their parent's backs. According to an email and video obtained exclusively by Okeefe Media Group, school counselor Fallon Corcoran references "Genesis," a student database that features a tiered ranking system to secretly classify students who want to transition without their parent's knowledge.

A source within the school recorded Fallon telling colleague Michael Schiff, "I had one of my students reach out to me about their preferred name for next year. Do we know how we can input their name into Genesis without it being visible by families?" Schiff replies, "I am not calling home… everything we talk about stays between us."

23. (2023) In an article titled, "Joe Biden is The Greatest Gift Ever to Iran's Ayatollahs," author DeRoy Murdock details Biden's enabling of Iran long before this $6 billion prisoner-swap payoff. Murdock cites the following as evidence of what informed Americans already knew.

Biden relaxed sanctions on Iran, while obsessively and immediately demolishing what President Trump had accomplished.

By letting the mullahs sell more oil, particularly to China (another international beauty), Iran's oil production swelled from 2.7 million barrels per day on December 31, 2020 – just before Trump departed – to 3.4 million barrels on May 31, 2023 – up 25.9%.

Biden's War on Domestic Oil hiked prices. This has gilded Tehran's coffers. Brent crude averaged $57.96 per barrel under Trump and $83.84 on Biden's watch, per the US Energy Information Administration. This increased Iran's oil revenue up 44.65%.

As Iran International reported, "Iranian oil shipments began to pick up toward the end of 2020, as candidate Joe Biden announced in September of that year his intention to revive the 2015 JCPOA," AKA the Iran-nuclear deal, which Trump correctly hurled atop the ash heap of history. Iran's exports subsequently soared from a low of 100,000 barrels per day in 2020, according to Reuters, to 1.5 million barrels in August – up 1,400%.

Former Director of National Intelligence John Ratcliffe tells Fox News Trey Gowdy, "Iran's access to foreign-exchange reserves went from $4 billion in the Trump administration to $72 billion in the Biden admin – up 1,700 %."

24. (2021) In a stunning shift The National Institutes of Health (NIH) admits to funding gain-of-function research on bat coronaviruses at China's Wuhan lab, despite Dr. Anthony Fauci repeatedly insisting to Congress that no such thing happened. As recently as last month, Fauci was accused of lying about gain-of-function research after documents, obtained by the Intercept, detailed grants given to EcoHealth Alliance for bat coronavirus studies.

In a letter to Representative James Comer (KY) Wednesday, a top NIH official blamed EcoHealth Alliance - the New York City-based nonprofit that has funneled US funds to the Wuhan lab - for not being transparent about the work it was doing.

NIH's principal deputy director, Lawrence A. Tabak, wrote in the letter that EcoHealth's "limited experiment" tested whether "spike proteins from naturally occurring bat coronaviruses circulating in China were capable of binding to the human ACE2 receptor in a mouse model." The lab mice infected with the modified virus "became sicker" than those that were given the unmodified virus, according to Tabak. "As sometimes occurs in science, this was an unexpected result of the research, as opposed to something that the researchers set out to do," Tabak said.

The admission from the NIH official directly contradicts Fauci's testimony to Congress in May and July, when he vehemently denied the US had funded gain-of-function projects in Wuhan at one point declaring, "I totally resent the lie you are now propagating."

A spokesman for Fauci said, despite the illuminating report, the good doctor has been "entirely truthful," in his testimony to Congress over whether a lab leak could have sparked the pandemic.

It is reported that a $3.1 million grant was awarded for a five-year period between 2014 and 2019. After the funding was renewed in 2019, it was suspended by the Trump administration in April 2020. The grant directed $599,000 to the Wuhan Institute of Virology for bat coronavirus research.

The proposal acknowledged the risks of such research, saying: "Fieldwork involves the highest risk of exposure to SARS or other CoVs, while working in caves with high bat density overhead and the potential for fecal dust to be inhaled."

Fauci has repeatedly clashed with Republican Sen. Rand Paul of Kentucky, who accused him of lying about the gain-of-function research. Paul erupted on Twitter following the emergence of the NIH letter, saying: "'I told you so' doesn't even begin to cover it here!"

25. (2023) "I demand that Congresswoman Rashida Tlaib be prevented from participating in any classified briefing about Israel's ongoing military operations, Israel's self-defense efforts, or any American military movements in and around the region."

Republican Ronny Jackson of Texas calls for penalties against Tlaib in a formal letter to the House leadership citing the fact that Tlaib has not condemned the beheadings of Israeli babies, her repeated promotion of debunked Hamas propaganda that falsely claimed Israel bombed a hospital, and her extensive history of anti-Semitism.

"We must not allow Hamas sympathizers in this body to serve as the mouthpiece for Palestinian terrorists," Jackson continued. "It has become clear that Congresswoman Tlaib's allegiance lies with Hamas, therefore she cannot be trusted with sensitive information."

Jackson adds that Tlaib's stance supporting Hamas and her anti-Israel position is reason enough to bar her from receiving classified updates on the war against Israel and demands that her security clearance be "revoked immediately!"

26. (2023) 'Et tu, Dana? "Anheuser-Busch and Bud Light were UFC's original beer sponsors more than fifteen years ago. I'm proud to announce we are back in business together. There are many reasons why I chose to go with Anheuser-Busch and Bud Light, most importantly because I feel we are very aligned when it comes to our core values and what the UFC brand stands for." UFC CEO Dana White announces the partnership between the UFC and Bud Light while extolling the shared "core values" between the two conglomerates. While Anheuser-Busch's arrangement with the UFC is reportedly worth upwards of $100 million, White assured Fox's Sean Hannity that the multi-year deal "was the furthest thing (from being) about money," during the interview.

UFC fans, however, apparently don't consider the Bud Light brand as representing their "core values" and quickly vent their disgust with the transaction online. No word as to whether or not transgender influencer and former Bud Lite spokesman, Dylan Mulvaney, plans to become a female UFC cage fighter.

27. (2017) "There is no excuse for this conduct. Hundreds of organizations were affected by these actions, and they deserve an apology from the IRS. We hope that today's settlement makes clear that this abuse of power will not be tolerated." The DOJ quotes Atty Gen Jeff Sessions chastising IRS officials while announcing two legal resolutions have been reached relating to the agency's transgressions.

In a legal settlement the IRS "expresses its sincere apology" for mistreating a conservative organization called Linchpins of Liberty (along with 40 other conservative groups) in their applications for tax-exempt status. In a second case, NorCal Tea Party Patriots and 427 other groups suing the IRS also reportedly reached a "substantial financial settlement" with the government.

28. (2023) "I wasn't allowed to say this then, but I just don't care now…back on 9/11, they wouldn't let us – at ABC News – wear a flag pin. I always thought that was wrong. I'm an American!" Chris Cuomo tells political scientist and commentator Ian Bremmer that ABC banned their reporters from wearing American flag pins or showing any "whiff" of patriotism from the airwaves following the 9/11 attacks."

Sadly, the admission surprises no one, as the mainstream media's anti-American sentiment has long been the rule rather than the exception.

29. (2023) The Daily Signal reports Manhattan Beach Middle School, Manhattan Beach, CA forced four Jewish students to remain silent after they became targets of anti-Semitic harassment and calls out administrators for now misusing a federal law to prevent anyone from holding them accountable.

The social media account Libs of TikTok post states that 4 Jewish students at MBMS were approached sometime after Hamas' Oct. 7 massacre of 1,400 civilians in Israel and were told "revenge is beautiful" and "all Israelis and Jews should be killed."

The 4 students to whom the vitriol was directed were then forced to sign a gag order preventing them from talking to anyone at the middle school or on social media about the hateful remarks and abuse.

Chillingly, the Manhattan Beach Unified School District concluded that the comments made to the Jewish students were "political and not hate speech," closing their investigation with what they described as "limited action."

The California Anti-Defamation League, which in July presented the Manhattan Beach school district with a "No Place for Hate" award for "leading the charge against bias, bullying, and hatred" issued a statement decrying the district's egregious series of actions in this incident. ADF called the actions of Manhattan Beach administrators "deeply hurtful" and a jeopardy to "the safety of the learning environment."

My Heritage Foundation colleague Roman Jankowski asked the Manhattan Beach School District to turn over emails from Jennifer Huynh, the principal of Manhattan Beach Middle School, regarding the verbal attack on the four Jewish students. In reply, the school district's public information officer, Hibah Samad, emailed an elusive and obstructive statement to Jankowski informing him that the district wouldn't release emails concerning the harassment of the students, details of the investigation, or what the investigation concluded.

The Manhattan Beach School District did inform The Daily Signal that administrators were "aware of recent allegations" concerning the anti-Semitic harassment of the 11-year-olds.

School district administrators characterized the harassment as "inappropriate interactions between students at MBMS surrounding their views on current events in the Middle East." Administrators then stonewalled releasing any other information by hiding behind the federal Family Education Rights and Privacy Act of 1974.

The school district maintained that gag orders signed by students are "normal," thereby confirming the need for "educators" to keep the leftist propaganda they are force-feeding impressionable children a secret from their parents.

30. (2023) After giving the chancellor of the State University System of Florida instructions to notify the University of Florida and the University of South Florida to deactivate their SJP (Students for Justice in Palestine) chapters, Governor Ron DeSantis states the decision has less to do with the First Amendment than it does with breaking laws pertaining to the provision of material support to terrorist organizations. "This is not cancel culture. This group, they themselves said in the aftermath of the Hamas attack, that they don't just stand in solidarity that they are part of this Hamas movement. And so you have a right to go out and demonstrate, but you can't provide material support to terrorism," DeSantis explained.

"And we also have strong laws in Florida against fundraising for groups like Hamas, and we are enforcing those vigorously," he added. "It's not a First Amendment issue. That's a material support to terrorism issue. So once you hitch your wagon to a group like Hamas, that takes you out of the realm of normal activity, and that's something that we're going to take action against. So we believe we're totally justified within the law," he concluded.

31. (2023) "When I am back in the White House, the United States will stand with Israel all the way - without hesitation, without qualification, and without apology. We will fully support the Israelis in their mission to ensure that Hamas is decimated, and these atrocities will be avenged. They will be avenged." President Trump acknowledges his full support for Israel in a speech in Las Vegas.

He continued, "Joe Biden's weakness caused the attack on Israel. Pure weakness and incompetence. Everywhere he goes, Biden's weakness provokes war and death because as history shows, evil only respects one thing: unyielding strength. You've got to be strong.

Otherwise, they're going to be taking over. When I am back in the White House, America's enemies will know once again if you try to kill our citizens, we will kill you. If you spill a drop of American blood, we spill a gallon of yours," Trump concluded.

NOVEMBER

1. (2023) When pressed by Fox News' Peter Doocy during a White House press briefing, National Security Council spokesman John Kirby says he "couldn't possibly answer" a question as to whether or not terrorists affiliated with Hamas have already crossed over the Mexican border into the US. "We are always concerned about the potential presence on U.S. soil of terrorists coming from overseas. That's something we're always worried about," Kirby initially said in an attempt to dodge the question.

As Kirby stammers on, Doocy points out that earlier in the day FBI Director Christopher Wray stated the terror threat to Americans has reached a "whole other level" due to Biden's open border. Unfortunately, Kamala Harris is not present and therefore unable to reassure Americans that she takes her job as "Border Czar" so seriously that one day she might even visit the border in person.

2. (2023) "What troubles me is the demonization of addiction, of human frailty, using me as its avatar and the devastating consequences it has for the millions struggling with addiction, desperate for a way out and being bombarded by the denigrating and near-constant coverage of me and my addiction on Fox News (more airtime than GOP presidential candidate Ron DeSantis) and in The New York Post (an average of *two stories a day* over the past year).

Desperate to blame his mounting legal woes on anyone and anything other than himself, Hunter Biden declares Fox News is actually responsible for his current predicament. Later, Rep. James Comer questions why money "earned" by Hunter ends up in the accounts of other Biden family members or why James Biden is paying back brother Joe's bank loans just days after getting a check from China.

Sadly, Hunter's crack addiction is actually the most likable thing about him.

3. (2023) In a video posted on X, VP Kamala Harris declares, "I am proud to announce the Biden Harris Administration will develop our nation's first national strategy to counter Islamophobia. This strategy will be a comprehensive and detailed plan to protect Muslims and those perceived to be Muslim from hate, bigotry, and violence and to address the concern that some government policies may discriminate against Muslims."
"Islamophobia Czar" Kamala Harris goes into damage control mode as

recent polls indicate a noticeable decline in Biden's support among Arab Americans incensed by US-supported air strikes on Gaza following the atrocities committed by Hamas' attack on innocent civilians on October 9.

The Anti-Defamation League report affirming a 388% rise in hate crimes being committed against Jews since Hamas' Oct 7 murderous rampage on Israeli civilians is apparently of no concern to the newly appointed Islamophobia Czar or her boss.

4. (2023) Marianne Malizia, director of the Air Force's Office of Diversity and Inclusion (SAF/DI) releases a newsletter celebrating the Air Force's DEI programming including the second annual Juneteenth celebration, LGBT+ representation at recruiting events, and the second annual Diversity, Equity, Inclusion and Accessibility Conference. Malizia reports the DEI agenda "soared to new heights" through holding or participating in major events, as the Department of Defense seeks to graft a DEI element "into all parts of the enterprise."

She also cited The Air Force's Barrier Analysis Working Groups, the LGBTQ+ Initiatives Team, which hosted a recruiting booth at the Capitol Pride Festival in Washington, D.C., on June 1, (and was even paid a personal visit by Sec of the Air Force, Frank Kendall). Red velvet cake was served at events as "a symbol of those who lost their lives during enslavement."

The Air Force failed to meet its recruiting targets for enlisted personnel and officers in the active duty, Reserve, and National Guard components in fiscal year 2023, the first time that has happened in more than two decades, a spokesperson previously told the DCNF.

No mention is made of the Air Force's new woke agenda possibly contributing to the drop in recruitment.

5. (2023) Indiana police arrest Ruba Almaghteh, 34, on charges of criminal recklessness after she intentionally slams her car into a building used by "The Israelite School of Universal and Practical Knowledge," which Ruba assumed was a school for Israeli children.

Almaghteh reportedly tells officers she was watching news coverage of the Israel-Hamas war on television and decided to attack the building because she was offended by the "Hebrew Israelite" symbol on the front of the building and confessed to the hate crime stating, "Yes. I did it on purpose."

Ironically, the Anti-Defamation League defines "The "Israelite School of Universal and Practical Knowledge as an "extreme and anti-Semitic" sect of the Black Hebrew Israelites. Additionally, The Southern Poverty Law Center has designated the Black Hebrew Israelites as an anti-Semitic hate group. Clearly, Ruba's violent attack was not very well thought out as her target turned out to be her like-minded Anti-Semitic homies.

6. (2022) During an episode of Sticher's "Naked Lunch" podcast, longtime late-night host Jimmy Kimmel claims he was willing to quit his job at ABC if his bosses asked him to stop making jokes about then-presidential hopeful Donald Trump.

Kimmel said the concern was "hinted at" by executives "right around the beginning of this whole Trump thing," when he says the network's research found he'd lost half of his fan base - maybe more"- as he began making more jokes about Trump.

"Ten years ago, among Republicans, I was the most popular talk show host. At least according to the research they did," Kimmel boasted. Research further reveals that ten years ago was around the last time Kimmel was funny.

7. (2003) "What Hamas did was horrific, and there's no justification for it. And what is also true is that the occupation, and what's happening to Palestinians, is unbearable. If you want to solve the problem, then you have to take in the whole truth and you then have to admit nobody's hands are clean, that all of us are complicit to some degree. "If you genuinely want to change this, then you've got to figure out how to speak to somebody on the other side and listen to them and understand what they are talking about and not dismiss it."

A duplicitous, desperate to be relevant, Barak Obama, talks out of both sides of his neck first stating "there is no justification" for Hamas' slaughtering of innocent Israeli civilians on Oct 8 then proceeding to actually list excuses for them. Obama's meddling immediately reminds Americans of why they don't miss him.

8. (2023) Hillary Clinton joins the brain trust of "The View" and cautions the co-hosts and audience to remember that "Adolf Hitler was duly elected," while warning of the Apocalypse that could occur if President Donald Trump is re-elected in 2024. Co-host Sunny Hostin asks Clinton about what might happen if Trump were to be elected in 2024, as he seeks a second term in office after losing in 2020. Clinton said she couldn't even think like that and added her tired refrain, "I think it would be the end of our country as we know it. He means to throw people in jail who disagree with him, shut down legitimate press outlets, do what he can to literally undermine the rule of law and our country's values," Clinton said, neglecting to add, "That's the Democrats' job!"

9. (2023) "I have uncovered screenshots from the X account of Dawn Marie Engoron, the wife of leftist NYC Judge Arthur Engoron who is overseeing the civil fraud trial of President Trump shows that she has been posting attacks on Trump from her account @dm-sminxs as the trial is ongoing.

This is an incredible bias. Less than 24 hours ago she posted tweets in which she said, "F*CK TRUMP!" She posted photo-shopped pics of President Trump in an orange jumpsuit, she attacked me during my Live show last night for exposing her husband, and she is openly attacking President Trump's lawyer! Judge Engoron needs to recuse himself and there needs to be a MISTRIAL in President Trump's NYC Civil Fraud Trial. This is some straight-up, third-world Banana Republic THUGGERY!!!"

Investigative journalist, Laura Loomer, blows the lid off Dawn Marie Engoron and her husband Judge Arthur Engoron's prejudice against President Trump as the latter defends himself against the latest politically contrived charges in the civil trial being heard before the smug Judge E.

One post included an AI-generated image of Trump bald in an orange prison jumpsuit next to one of an old lady scrawling "F*ck Trump" on a brick wall.

Dawn Marie later denies making social media posts attacking President Trump in a statement to *Newsweek*.

According to the rules of the Chief Administrative Judge of the New York State Unified Court System, judges must "not allow family, social, political or other relationships to influence their judicial conduct or judgment." These are Constitutional rights of all defendants (unless their name is Donald Trump).

10. (2023) It's reported that in her highly anticipated memoir *"My Name is Barbra,"* 81-year-old Barbra Streisand calls former President Donald Trump "completely unfit" to be commander in chief while simultaneously gushing over her friends Bill and Hillary Clinton, labeling them "the most appealing couple."

"Yes, I have opinions. And it is my right to express them, just like any other citizen," she wrote. "Actually, I think it's our responsibility," she remarked before adding that "artists can serve as the "conscience of the country."

Yes, Babs if there is one thing Americans need right now it is more lecturing courtesy of self-aggrandizing, low-information, elitist Hollywood dummies.

11. (2023) Joe Biden reportedly calls former Obama adviser David Axelrod a "prick" behind closed doors after Axelrod questioned if it is "wise" for Biden to continue down his re-election path as poll after poll continues to highlight Americans' concerns over his age and ability to beat current GOP frontrunner, Donald Trump.

Politico columnist Jonathan Martin later writes, "Calling David Axelrod a prick is not a strategy to win 270 electoral votes. And repeating a PG version of the same animus in public while litigating polling with the White House press corps also won't make Biden's reelection any likelier."

It's an awkward situation, Joe, but to be perfectly fair – you are both "pricks!"

12. (2008) "… Hillary Clinton is a brittle, relentless manipulator with few stable core values who shuffles through useful personalities like a card shark." Feminist Camille Paglia weighs in on the fraud that is Hillary Clinton.

13. (2023) After a group of asylum seekers are relocated by bus to Floyd Bennett Field in Brooklyn, part of a national park that has been refashioned and set up with tents to accommodate 2,000 migrants, the plan immediately backfires when the indignant itinerants make it clear the park is an insult and unacceptable. NY Assemblywoman Jaime Williams, who represents the district where the field is located, sounds stunned as she films the migrants getting off the blue Metropolitan Transportation Authority bus, walking past the main entrance to the complex then walking straight onto another bus headed back to Manhattan.

One migrant said he was going to head back to the lavish Roosevelt Hotel - which has been commandeered by the Dem mayor - while another angrily told the NY Post: "My kids go to school in the Bronx. For us to live out here is ridiculous." When Williams questioned one of the officials about what had just gone on, he reportedly told her that he would explain after she turned off her camera.

Plainly, immigrants who have broken into the country have standards that American taxpayers had better meet if they know what's good for them.

14. (2023) Two years after being sentenced to prison for his role in the Jan 6 US Capitol riot, folk hero "QAnon Shaman," Jacob Chansley, reportedly files paperwork signaling his interest in running for the Arizona congressional seat being vacated by Debbie Lesko (R).

Chansley, 35, gained notoriety for his horned fur hat, bare chest, and face paint that made him one of the most recognizable Jan. 6 protestors. He pleaded guilty to a charge of obstructing an official proceeding and was sentenced to 41 months in prison. Prosecutors sought the harshest of sentences for "QS" in an attempt to "set an example" for the future trials of jailed citizens while deeming him "emblematic of the barbaric crowd."

The Arizona Republic reports a candidate statement of interest was signed by Jacob Angeli-Chansley and filed with the Arizona Secretary of State's Office on Thursday, indicating he would seek to run as a Libertarian. He has also been known to go by Jacob Angeli. - Vote QS 2024!!!

15. (2023) It's time to call an "insurrection" an "insurrection!" A mob of 150 anti-Semitic "insurrectionists" stormed the entrance to the DNC headquarters, leading to clashes with Capitol Police and forcing the evacuation of several members of Congress inside. At the time of the "insurrection," 7 members of Congress were inside when they were ordered to evacuate by Capitol Police. Congressman Brad Sherman reported he could hear the "insurrectionist's" chants of "ceasefire now," referring to the "insurrectionists" opposition to Israel's retaliation in the aftermath of Hamas" slaughter of 1,200 innocent men, women, children and babies on October 7th.

On October 18th, a crowd of "insurrectionists" stormed the Capitol following a rally in which Rashida Tlaib whipped the "insurrectionists" into a frenzy with lies about the destruction of a hospital in Gaza, falsely blaming

Israel for the incident. Then, on November 4th, hundreds more "insurrectionists" stormed the fence of the White House, smearing red paint on the brick columns and attacking Secret Service agents. It is unlikely any "insurrectionists" arrested at the scenes of these "insurrections" will face any consequences for their "insurrection" unlike the dozens of Jan 6 protestors being held in squalid conditions in the Washington DC jail.

16. (2023) At a press conference Gavin Newsom acknowledged that the recent cleanup efforts in San Francisco were timed to coincide with the arrival of "fancy" leaders (Xi Jinping) for the annual Asia-Pacific Economic Cooperation leaders' summit. He adds, "San Francisco has been struggling to shed its image as a city in decline. I know folks say, Oh, they're just cleaning up this place because all those fancy leaders are coming into town. That's true because it's true," Newsom admits. "But it's also true, for months and months and months prior to APEC, we've been having different conversations. And we've raised the bar of expectation between the city, the county, and the state, and our federal partners as well that we all have to do more and do better."

"Governor Newsom orders homeless camps removed in San Francisco in an obvious attempt to impress his new best friend, China's Communist dictator Xi Jinping," Melissa Melendez, a former California state senator posted on X. Another person posted that Newsom "unapologetically" admitted that he "only cleaned up San Francisco because (Xi) is coming to town—what he failed to explain is where all the homeless people are now..."

An anonymous source states Newsom says not to worry as the hundreds of evicted homeless drug addicts are being well cared for and are currently in the process of being registered as Democrats.

17. (2021) Taliban forces hold a military parade in Kabul using captured American-made armored vehicles and Russian helicopters in a display that shows their ongoing transformation from an insurgent force to a regular standing army. The Taliban operated as an insurgent fighter for two decades but have used the large stock of weapons and equipment left behind by Joe Biden in August to "overhaul" their forces. The parade was linked to the graduation of 250 freshly trained soldiers, the Taliban defense ministry spokesman said.

The exercise involved dozens of US-made M117 armored security vehicles driving slowly up and down a major Kabul road with MI-17 helicopters patrolling overhead. Many soldiers carried American-made M4 assault rifles. Most of the weapons and equipment the Taliban forces are now using are those supplied by Washington to the American-backed government in Kabul in a bid to construct an Afghan national force capable of fighting the Taliban.

Those forces melted away with the fleeing of Afghan President Ashraf Ghani from Afghanistan – leaving the Taliban to take over major military assets.

Taliban officials have said that pilots, mechanics, and other specialists from the former Afghan National Army would be integrated into a new force, which has also started wearing conventional military uniforms in place of the traditional Afghan clothing normally worn by their fighters.

According to a report late last year by the Special Inspector General for Afghanistan Reconstruction (Sigar), the US government transferred to the Afghan government more than $28 billion worth of defense articles and services, including weapons, ammunition, vehicles, night-vision devices, aircraft, and surveillance systems, from 2002 to 2017. Ironically, for the Taliban, every day of Joe Biden's presidency has been like Christmas for them.

18. (2023) "Before we get going, are there any Moms for Liberty in the house? Moms for Liberty? No? Good. Then hands will not need to be thrown tonight." While hosting one of the oldest and most prestigious literary awards in the US, Reading Rainbow star Levar Burton, 66, threatens physical violence against women who compose the conservative group "Moms for Liberty."

The parental rights group, formed in response to onerous COVID restrictions in schools, was labeled an extremist group by the far-left Southern Poverty Law Center, which announced they plan to sue for defamation.

Moms for Liberty later responds to Burton's remarks on X writing, "American moms weep as a childhood favorite, Reading Rainbow, calls for physical attacks against us because we are protecting the innocence of our children. @levarburton, why have you sunk so low? Threatening physical violence against women?" Note to Jordy: Many women in Moms for Liberty are badasses and you no longer have a "phaser," so quit running your mouth.

19. (2023) House Speaker Mike Johnson announces that nearly all of the surveillance footage from the Jan. 6, 2021, Capitol incursion will be released and some of the initially released video showed non-violent protesters moving freely through the Capitol with Capitol Police monitoring the situation, but seemingly not too concerned. Officers weren't directing people out of the building, though there was an exit door right behind police.

In other surveillance footage posted on social media, Capitol Police officers release a man who had been taken into custody who then turns around and fist-bumps the officers before heading out of the Capitol. The videos stand in stark contrast to the footage the January 6 Committee and the legacy media aired on a loop for public consumption for years.

The videos prove the vast majority of those who protested on Jan. 6 were simply exercising their First Amendment rights to "peaceably assemble, and to petition the Government for a redress of grievances." Leftists are quick to point out that Constitutional rights apply only to them and do not protect President Trump or his legions of supporters.

20. (2023) "We just obtained Customs and Border Patrol agency documents directing personnel to only use woke language to avoid "misgendering" individuals crossing into the United States."

A tweet from the Oversight Project at the Heritage Foundation details an order from border chief Alejandro Mayorkas directing border guards to ignore the biological distinction between the two complementary sexes and instead orders them to submit to the political claim that each person's "gender" is more important than their biological sex." Essentially agents must allow people to sneak across the border under the disguise of "transgender" pronouns."

Biden's directive to Mayorkas goes on to clarify the new protocol, which orders border guards not to presume the correct sex and corresponding pronouns for illegal migrants. The instructions say:

If a longer dialogue (with a migrant) is occurring, it may be appropriate to ask the individual their preferred pronoun.

For example, state "I would like to be respectful — what name and pronoun would you like me to use when addressing you"?

Avoid asking 'What is your sex?" unless operationally necessary.

DO NOT: Use "he, him, she, her" pronouns until you have more information about, or provided by, the individual.

American citizens can finally breathe a sigh of relief knowing Biden and Mayorkas have addressed the primary concern with the mass invasion occurring at the Southern border – that being "misgendering" the terrorists, MS-13 gang members, and pedophiles who are breaking into the country.

21. (1970) "I would pray that if you understood what communism was, you would hope, you would pray on your knees that we would someday become communists." "Hanoi Jane" Fonda extols the virtues of communism during a speech at Michigan State University.

22. (2023) Outrage ensues after special counsel investigating Joe Biden's documents scandal reports no charges will be filed in the case. Special counsel Robert Hur's report is expected to sharply criticize Biden and his aides for their handling of classified documents - the standard treatment for the protected establishment class.

Hur's investigation, which began in January following his appointment by Attorney General Merrick Garland, has spanned nearly a year. It has involved interviews with around 100 Biden aides, including the President's embattled son, Hunter Biden, who himself faces unrelated legal troubles following an indictment on federal gun charges. Biden himself was interviewed last month.

"The president has been interviewed as part of the investigation being led by Hur," reads the statement from the White House Counsel's Office spokesperson Ian Sams (the same person who lied and melted down over Hunter Biden's $260K in Chinese wires).

Of note, Hunter Biden listed Joe's Wilmington, Delaware, home – where a bunch of classified documents were found – as his address when he received above mentioned Chinese wires, due to the Biden family's dealings with CCP-linked businessmen.

As Jonathan Turley, a nationally recognized legal scholar previously noted, the most glaring problem is that, after they were removed at the end of his term as vice president, the documents were repeatedly moved and divided up. Some were found in the Penn Center office used by Biden in Washington, D.C. Others were found in his garage and reportedly in his library.

Biden made clear from the beginning that he expected the investigation to be perfunctory and brief. He publicly declared that he has "no regrets" over his own conduct and told the public that the documents investigation would soon peter out when it determined that "there is no there there."

Additionally, it appears that a critical claim by the White House in the scandal may not only be false but was knowingly false at the time it was made. The White House and Biden's counsel have long maintained that, as soon as documents were discovered in the D.C. office, they notified the national archives. Many asked why they did not immediately call the FBI, to which Team Biden explained it was because, unlike Trump, they took immediate action to notify authorities. An inane explanation that only makes sense to the lobotomized residents living in "Bidenland." While puzzling, Biden's weaponized FBI would undoubtedly have run interference for him in the same manner as his (sham) special counsel.

Meanwhile, Biden's DOJ is doing all within its power to imprison former President Trump over classified documents he did have the authority to declassify but Biden does not even receive a slap on the wrist for mishandling and keeping classified documents he kept as a VP and Senator when he was not allowed to declassify them.

23. (2021) "I'd like to suggest to everybody out there, come out to your family this Thanksgiving. Just come out. See what happens." During an episode of "The View" resident Life Coach Joy Behar offers up some advice for gays, suggesting that when talking politics over Thanksgiving dinner, those who haven't come out to their families yet do so. Unfortunately, all did not appreciate Behar's unsolicited sharing of her wisdom.

One person tweeted, "How dare you take a very important and sensitive moment in someone who is part of the LGBTQIA Community & turn it into a joke? Some have been shunned from their family because of it. Not a joke. Be ashamed."

CNN reached out to reps for Behar for comment but received none. Behar has felt no shame for her dozens of prior gaffes - it is doubtful she will feel any for this one. Just add it to her growing list of "Stupidest Things Anyone, Anywhere Has Ever Said."

24. (2023) United Talent Agency drops Susan Sarandon as a client following remarks she made over the weekend in relation to the Israel-Hamas war. "There are a lot of people afraid of being Jewish at this time and are getting a taste of what it feels like to be a Muslim in this country, so often subjected to violence," the actress said at a rally in New York City's Union Square, comparing that experience to the erosion of safety many Jews feel in the US amid rising anti-Semitism.

Asra Nomani, a Muslim American journalist, set Sarandon straight, posting on X and refuting the implied assumptions underlying Sarandon's comments. "Please don't minimize the experience of Jewish Americans by sanitizing the hell that it is for Muslims living in Muslim countries and vilifying America for the life - and freedoms - she offers Muslims like my family," Nomani tweeted, describing the rules that constrain women's daily lives in many Muslim-governed countries. "Go, live like a Muslim woman in a Muslim country. You will come back to America and kiss the land beneath your feet."

Better yet, Susan, just leave and stay gone! You have been unhappy in America for a long time, and you really deserve to live as a woman in any Muslim country you desire!

25. (2023) "Martha, I'm not saying this is accurate, but I can read a poll and the American people have concluded that President Biden is old, and he needs soup and an early bedtime, and they have concluded that Vice President Harris is not capable, that when her IQ gets to 75, she should sell."

Esteemed Sen John Kennedy rips Kamala Harris, saying the American people have decided she is "not capable." Kennedy cites the state of the U.S.-Mexico border crisis, inflation, crime, and conflicts in Ukraine and Gaza while delivering the blistering assessment of the performances of both Kamala and Joe Biden. "Since President Biden and Vice President Harris have been in office about 8.4 million people have come into our country illegally. That's four Nebraskas," Kennedy continued. "We don't have the slightest idea who they are. Why is that? Because this administration believes in open borders. Why is that? Because this administration has embraced the neo-socialist woke-wing, loon-wing of the Democratic Party," the good Senator concluded.

VP Harris reportedly did not respond to the Daily Caller News Foundation's request for comment.

26. (2023) "It's just unbelievable how much he's degenerated just during his time in office. We cannot afford to have this man in office for the remainder of this term and then (for) another four years after that. He's already putting us at great risk right now." Former White House physician Ronny Jackson warns that Joe Biden is currently suffering from cognitive decline, which has accelerated during his time in office.

Jackson had previously demanded Biden take a cognitive test and release its results to the public. The White House and Democrats have ignored those calls, claiming that Biden is in perfect health. Republicans have frequently commented on Biden's slurred speaking patterns, his frequent bouts with confusion, and his overall appearance, which "comes off as weak, sluggish, and detached from reality." It appears that every day more and more Dems are agreeing with Jackson's assessment of Joe Biden.

27. (2023) With everything plaguing the world, war in the Middle East, inflation, mortgage rates, astronomically high gas prices, general world unrest, and a historically unpopular president, Democrats have become anxious to distract voters leading up to the 2024 election.

Enter Dem Sen Elizabeth Warren who points out the biggest concern for voters should be (drumroll, please) "the sandwich shop monopoly." Fortunately, Liz is on it stating, "The FTC is right to investigate whether the purchase of Subway by the same firm that owns Jimmy John's and McAlister's Deli creates a sandwich monopoly. "We don't need another private equity deal that could lead to higher food (subway sandwich) prices for consumers," Warren wrote on X.

The private equity firm's holdings prompted the Federal Trade Commission (FTC) to launch a probe earlier this month to examine whether the deal gives the company a monopoly over sandwich shops and other brands in the fast-food industry, according to a report by Politico. Americans can rest easier knowing that the self-appointed Sandwich Czar is on patrol.

28. (2023) The mother of a 9-year-old KC Chief's football fan who wore a headdress and painted his face red and black to a Kansas City Chiefs game blasts "Deadspin" for accusing the boy of "doubling up" on racism against black and Native communities - noting that her son is himself Native American.

Holden Armenta became an unexpected focus of an article by senior writer Carron Phillips that focused on a photo of the boy standing sideways, suggesting he was wearing blackface with no mention of the red side.

"The NFL needs to speak out against the Kansas City Chiefs fan in Black face, Native headdress," read the headline, which accused the boy of "doubling up on the racism." Phillips, a former New York Daily News reporter also slammed Holden's Native American headdress and his "Tomahawk Chop" gesture, claiming the boy "found a way to hate Black people and Native Americans at the same time."

"It takes a lot to disrespect two groups of people at once," Carron wrote apparently oblivious to the fact that he has accomplished it with relative ease. "This is what happens when you ban books, stand against Critical Race Theory, and try to erase centuries of hate," he wrote. "You give future generations the ammunition they need to evolve and recreate racism better than before."

The boy's outraged mother, Shannon Armenta, shared numerous images of her son getting a warm reception at the game while suggesting Deadspin focused on a photo that hid the fact that half her son's face was painted red. "This has nothing to do with the NFL," she wrote, suggesting the photo was picked purely "to create division."

In fact, the Post Millennial reports Holden's grandfather, Raul Armenta, sits on the board of the Chumash Tribe in Santa Ynez, California, and is listed as a "business committee member" who was first elected to the board in 2016 on the tribe's website. "Raul looks forward to continuing the legacy of building a solid economic foundation for future generations of the Chumash tribe, it reads."

Instead of issuing an immediate apology to the boy, his father, Chief's fans, Native Americans, and all other folks he has managed to vilify and offend, Phillips (astoundingly) doubles down on his claim in this since-deleted X post.

"For the idiots in my mentions who are treating this as some harmless act because the other side of his face was painted red, I could make the argument that it makes it even worse," he wrote in the post, according to the Post Millennial. "Y'all are the ones who hate Mexicans but wear sombreros on Cinco (de Mayo). "If the NFL had outlawed the chop at Chiefs games and been more aggressive in changing the team's name, then we wouldn't be here," Carron blathers on. The most obvious problem with his assessment is that prejudice will continue to flourish as long as racist vermin (him) are allowed to promote it under the guise of journalism.

No comment has been made in defense of the 9-year-old fan by Roger Goodell, the Chiefs, or Taylor Swift thus far. On top of disgracing himself, journalism, and humanity, Carron's shameful actions revitalize the "Make Deadspin Dead Again" movement.

29. (2023) "It's the duplicity of the Democrats, the hypocrisy. We're not stupid. The brothers are not stupid. We understand when someone's for us and when someone is not, and it's obvious that the Democratic Party is not for us." Mark Fisher, co-founder of Black Lives Matter Rhode Island, joins Lawrence Jones on "Fox and Friends" to discuss why some Black voters are abandoning Democrats in favor of President Trump in the 2024 presidential election.

"We've been used and abused for so long by that party, they don't value our vote," Fisher said. "Their policies are basically racist policies. I believe it's a racist party. Donald Trump is just the opposite. He's going to tell you how it is. He's going to give it to you straight."

"A lot of people are misinformed," Fisher continued. "They don't really understand because they don't educate themselves on Donald Trump as a person and his history, but if they do that, and it's going to take educated leaders to get the word out there, I think that it'll happen on its own, and it'll be organic, because personally, I love the man."

Note: Fisher's endorsement of President Trump is the first step BLM has taken to actually help Black people since the organization's inception in July 2013.

30 (2023) The Post Millennial reveals a new interim report compiled by the House Republicans' Committee on Homeland Security shows American taxpayers will be forced to cover $451 billion in aid to illegal immigrants as

a result of Joe Biden's open border policies. The expenses come in the form of hotel rooms, food, clothing, busing, flight, and other benefits states have been giving to migrants that are being covered by federal tax dollars.

The report states that only a small fraction of the money will be recouped from the taxes paid by illegal aliens, with the rest falling on the shoulders of American taxpayers. Democrat voters are reportedly shocked to learn that they too, will be on the hook for the astronomical tax liability insisting they had assumed it would be paid for solely by Republicans.

DECEMBER

1. (2023) "It feels like young Americans don't have the same sense of patriotism and love for the USA that was commonplace not that long ago. Now, people are being taught to hate America and that the USA is the bad guy. The consequences are brutal. We have people in America praising and siding with Osama bin Laden. It's hard to believe it's real, but unfortunately, it 100% is. UFC President Dana White lashes out at young Americans who don't love the USA.

White continues, "If you look at all the sh*t that's going on in the world right now. If we went to war, there's no respect for the police anymore. There's no respect for the military. Our country. Our way of life that we have here. You can sit around, and nit-pick and talk about things that are wrong with the United States. Let me tell you something. I'm going to tell f*cking your generation, my generation, everybody's generation. This is it. So, all these f*cking people who are like, 'Oh God, if President Trump wins, I'm leaving the country.' They all say it. Nobody f*cking does it!"

Note to Dana: If you are trying to make amends for rekindling the UFC's relationship with the wokeists at Bud Lite, congrats and "mission accomplished!" This is the Dana White we have come to know and love!

2. (2023) Appellate Court Justices David Navarro and Mary Ellen Coghlan rule that actor Jussie Smollett's rights were not violated when Special prosecutor Dan Webb was appointed to find out why the office of Cook County State's Attorney Kim Foxx initially dropped his hate hoax case.

In 2021 the disgraced "Empire" actor was accused of fabricating a racist and homophobic attack against himself in 2019, then deceiving the Chicago police about it. He was found guilty by a jury on five out of six felony counts of disorderly conduct for staging a hate crime and trying to implicate President Trump and MAGA supporters as being the perpetrators, including accusing them of placing a noose around his neck.

Initially, Smollett had reported to police that he was attacked by two people wearing ski masks while walking home late at night after buying a sandwich from Subway. "When he got up and went into his apartment building, he still had that Subway sandwich with him," Johnson said, pointing out that victims of assault typically drop what they're carrying because they're afraid.

"This guy had the sandwich in his hand, never been touched," he concluded.

Smollett was initially sentenced to a slap on the wrist of 150 days in jail but was sprung by his lawyers after only serving six days when they filed an appeal. His lawyers contested various aspects of the case, including the role of a special prosecutor, jury selection, and presented evidence, among other arguments.

Neither Smollett nor his defenders have issued apologies for the hoax.

After losing his appeal the court affirmed his disorderly conduct conviction and Smollett was reportedly ordered back to jail to serve the remainder of his time. Well played, Jussie, well played indeed.

3. (2023) When CNN's Dana Bash asks Rep. Pramila Jayapal, D-Wash why it is so difficult for progressives to "unequivocally call out the barbaric sexual violence being committed by Hamas' terrorists against Israeli women," Jayapal, who chairs the left-wing Congressional Progressive Caucus, does not answer and, instead, immediately turns the conversation back to Israel. "With respect, I was just asking about the women, and progressive women's groups on Hamas' use of rape as a weapon of war. With respect, I was just asking about the women, and you turned it back to Israel. I'm asking you about Hamas," Bash pointed out.

The lawmaker replied that she had already answered the question and added, "We have to be balanced about bringing in the outrages against Palestinians. Fifteen thousand Palestinians have been killed in Israeli air strikes, three-quarters of whom are women and children."

Representative Ritchie Torres (D) later tells Bash, "Look, there's often been a double standard against Israel when it comes to condemning the sheer butchery and barbarism of Hamas. Public officials have a moral obligation to speak with clarity rather than caveats. And I found it deeply troubling, for example, that the UN Women, the so-called women's rights arm of the United Nations, went 50 days without commenting on or condemning the sexual atrocities that Hamas perpetrated against Israeli women. For me, this is not about politics. This is about decency. It is indecent to deny or downplay or 'both sides' the rape and sexual violence against Israeli women on October 7."

Other Democrats, including Reps. Debbie Wasserman Schultz, D-Fla., and Debbie Dingell, D-Mich., also criticized Jayapal's comments. "Hamas terrorists raped Israeli women and girls. The only 'balanced' approach is to condemn sexual violence loudly, forcefully, and without exceptions. Outrageous for anyone to 'both sides' sexual violence," Schultz wrote on social media.

4. (2023) Following revelations that the Federal Air Marshal Service has monitored individuals who traveled to Washington, D.C. on Jan. 6, 2021, former marshal Sonya Hightower-LaBosco informs Glenn Beck that a newborn baby is on the "terrorist watch list" and is being monitored by DHS due to the infant's father's involvement in the Jan. 6, 2021, protests.

Hightower-LaBosco goes on to discuss how federal air marshals were furious as they were reassigned to assist along the southern border along with being tasked to investigate individuals linked to Jan. 6. She calls it a "shocking debacle" that air marshals were not performing duties that align with their specialized training to "thwart hijackings" in the air.

"We're down on the border doing non-law enforcement duties; handing out water, driving people to the hospital, waiting for them to get stitches to bring them back to the Border Patrol facilities," the executive director of the Air Marshal's National Council briefed Beck.

She returned to Beck's program the next day to discuss the mind-numbing use of air marshals to monitor a baby: "This 8-week-old baby is on the terrorist watch list. And it's not just one air marshal that will be assigned. It's a minimum of three," she revealed. "You will have three air marshals following this 8-week-old baby. No matter if the baby travels with the grandparents. If the baby just travels with cousins. It doesn't matter. Once the baby is on the list, by their name, the baby is going to stay on that list."

The infant's father was allegedly charged for entering the Capitol on January 6, 2021. Hightower-LaBosco explained that the man's fiancée and baby in question were flying to Puerto Rico to visit family when it was revealed that the child was on the terror watch list. It is important to note that, at the time of the alleged crime by the baby's father, the baby had not yet been conceived.

5. (2023) "We are seeing and beginning to pay attention and to count and record the deaths that are related to climate and those deaths are being meticulously tallied and are already at a high and growing body count."

Hillary Clinton tells attendees at the 28th annual UN climate conference in Dubai that climate change-related deaths are at an all-time high, are gender and equity-influenced, and are being "meticulously counted."

Particularly cringe-worthy is Hillary's use of the phrase "high and growing body count," which has been used to describe the mounting death toll of highly suspicious deaths of perfectly healthy people linked to the Clintons.

6. (1999) During a "60 Minutes" interview Al Gore declares he used to hypnotize chickens when he was a kid. When reached for comment the chickens insist it was the other way around.

7. (2023) "If my testimony makes me transphobic, then I believe your opening monologue makes you a misogynist." During testimony on Capitol Hill former University of Kentucky swimmer Riley Gaines, delivered a knockout blow to Dem Rep. Summer Lee of Pennsylvania after the latter said, "Although the title of this hearing implies a much-needed discussion, we're likely going to be forced to listen to transphobic bigotry."

8. (2023) "Hunter Biden "spent millions of dollars on an extravagant lifestyle rather than paying his tax bills." Special counsel David Weiss reports on Hunter Biden's lapse in memory in failing to pay on at least $1.4 million owed between 2016 and 2019, a period where he has acknowledged struggling with addiction. The back taxes have since been paid. If convicted, Hunter Biden, 53, could receive a maximum of 17 years in prison. "The special counsel probe remains open," Weiss said.

"First Son" Hunter Biden is indicted on nine tax charges in California as a special counsel investigation into the business dealings of President Joe Biden's son intensifies against the backdrop of the 2024 election. The new charges filed include three felonies and six misdemeanors and are in addition to federal firearms charges in Delaware alleging Hunter Biden broke laws against drug users having guns in 2018. They come after a "sweetheart" plea deal collapsed over the summer that would have spared him jail time, putting the case on track to a possible trial as his father campaigns for reelection.

"Based on the facts and the law, if Hunter's last name was anything other than Biden, the charges in Delaware, and now California, would not have been brought," defense attorney Abbe Lowell said in a statement. Remarkably, Lowell kept a straight face while admonishing the prosecution.

9. (2021) In a video excerpt an emotional Hillary Clinton delivers what would have been her 2016 "victory speech" to viewers.

"My fellow Americans, today you've sent a message to the whole world," Clinton says. "Our values endure, our democracy stands strong, and our motto remains 'E pluribus Unum.' Out of many, one. We will not be defined only by our differences. We will not be an us vs. them country. The American dream is big enough for everyone."

Clinton talks about what she describes as a "long, hard campaign" through which the country was "challenged to choose between two very different visions for America. Fundamentally, this election challenged us to decide what it means to be an American in the 21st century," she says.

"Today with your children on your shoulders, neighbors at your side, friends old and new standing as one, you renewed our democracy. And because of the honor you have given me, you changed its face forever. I've met women who were born before women had the right to vote. They've been waiting 100 years for tonight. I've met little boys and girls who didn't understand why a woman has never been president before. Now they know, and the world knows, that in America every boy and every girl can grow up to be whatever they dream, even president of the United States," she says.

Agreed, Hillary it's just that Americans would prefer if their first female POTUS hadn't been one of the architects of Benghazi!

10. (2021) "They were involuntarily separated for failing to follow the lawful order to receive the Covid-19 vaccine." Air Force spokeswoman Ann Stefanek tells CNN the Air Force has discharged 27 service members for refusing to get the COVID-19 vaccine.

The Air Force had the earliest deadline for vaccination, requiring its service members to be fully vaccinated by November 2. Members of the Air Force Reserve and Air National Guard had until December 2. Stefanek said it is unclear whether any of the 27 service members were Space Force Guardians. All the members were in their first enlistments and had served less than six years, so their requests for vaccine exemptions did not go to a board, she said.

In addition, Stefanek reported service members discharged for refusing to get the vaccine might be required to repay any unearned special or incentive pay.

11. (2023) 511 Harvard faculty sign a letter in support of its president, Claudine Gay, despite intense blowback and calls for her firing after she failed to condemn calls for the genocide of Jews.

The support comes as a statement is expected to be made about Gay's future, just days after University of Pennsylvania president Liz Magill lost her job over similar testimony failing to condemn antisemitism, The Harvard Crimson" reported.

The 700-plus faculty members signed a letter Sunday to the Harvard Corporation urging the university to allow Gay to remain at her post as billboard trucks circled the campus with signs reading "Fire Gay."

Despite the outrage, the faculty members said they "urge you in the strongest possible terms to defend the independence of the university and to resist political pressures that are at odds with Harvard's commitment to academic freedom, including calls for the removal of President Claudine Gay. The critical work of defending a culture of free inquiry in our diverse community cannot proceed if we let its shape be dictated by outside forces," they added in the letter obtained by the student paper."

In response to the backlash over her testimony, Gay issued an apology for her remarks stating, "I am sorry. Words matter. When words amplify distress and pain, I don't know how you could feel anything but regret."

12. (2023) Fox News reports a surge of migrants crossing the southern border is overwhelming agents who are now outnumbered by alien crossers (mostly single males) by a ratio of 200 to 1, including 5,000 per day. It is projected that, by the end of the year, 1,825,000 immigrants will have crossed into the country. Since October 30 of those crossers were on the "Terror Watch List." The astounding numbers do not include the estimated 1.7 million "gotaways" who have evaded apprehension since 2021.

13. (2023) "What they're trying to do is they're trying to kill me, knowing that it will be a pain greater than my father could be able to handle, and so therefore destroying a presidency in that way. I realized that it's not about me. And then the second thing that I realized is that these people are just sad, very, very sick people that have most likely just faced traumas in their

that they've decided that they are going to turn into an evil that they decide that they're going to inflict on the rest of the world." Victim Hunter Biden joins musician Moby on his podcast, "Moby Pod," telling his truth following his second indictment on tax crimes in California.

14. (2022) The US Department of Energy's Loan Programs Office announces that it is issuing a $2.5 billion loan to help start three lithium battery manufacturing hubs in Ohio, Tennessee, and Michigan.

In October Joe Biden introduced the American Battery Materials Initiative, which the White House has called "a new effort to mobilize the entire government and securing a reliable and sustainable supply of critical minerals used for power, electricity and electric vehicles." At the same time, the Administration pledged $2.8 billion from the bipartisan infrastructure law passed last year to 20 manufacturing and processing companies for projects in 12 states.

No mention is made of the ecological damage caused by mining lithium, which consumes significant amounts of water and energy and can pollute the air and water with chemicals and heavy metals. In addition, mining lithium can disrupt wildlife habitats and cause soil erosion, leading to long-term ecological damage.

15. (2020) "I know everyone wants to get back to the time when Christmas was a situation where you could have many, many guests indoors, congregating, having fun together," Dr. Fauci tells CNN's Wolf Blitzer. But "the situation is different now," he said. If Americans disregard the dire situation already underway and travel for the holidays anyway, Fauci warned that it "could be a very difficult January."

Dr. Fauci clarifies his position that he doesn't want to cancel Christmas he just needs people to be more careful. The high number of holiday travelers during the pandemic has the nation's top infectious disease expert worried.

"As you might imagine, it's quite concerning to me," he said. "This type of travel is risky, particularly if people start congregating when they get to their destination in large crowds, in indoor settings. I'm afraid that if, in fact, we see this happen, we will have a surge that's superimposed upon the difficult situation we are already in. So, it could be a very difficult January coming up if these things happen."

Fauci said whenever he talks about being careful as the coronavirus pandemic rages across the country, he's accused of wanting to "cancel Christmas." While Fauci appears to view himself as a historical figure on the level of Jesus, he is surprised to learn he doesn't have the power to cancel the celebration of our Savior's birth.

16. (2020) During an appearance on The Late Show with Stephen Colbert, Dr. Jill Biden reports being surprised by a newspaper op-ed piece suggesting she stop using the "Dr." title before her name.

"That was such a surprise," she said, seated next to her husband, President-elect Joe Biden. "It was really the tone of it … He called me 'kiddo.' One of the things that I'm most proud of is my doctorate. I mean, I worked so hard for it."

"Jill Biden has a doctorate in education. Last week, Joseph Epstein wrote in the Wall Street Journal that Biden should drop the honorific because she is not a medical doctor. Epstein wrote that her use of the title "feels fraudulent, not to say a touch comic."

Epstein's article received backlash from some calling it sexist. Others defended it. Biden received her doctorate from the University of Delaware in 2007, according to her official biography. She is usually addressed in public with the "Dr." honorific, and official documents typically include it before her name.

CNN's longtime policy refers only to medical doctors as "Dr." in its reporting. That's also the policy of the Associated Press, whose style guide is widely used by news agencies the world over.

When Colbert asked Joe for his opinion on the subject Biden should have said, "C'mon, man! If they can call me "president" they sure as hell can call her "doctor!"

17. (2022) In another big victory for criminals, NYPD agrees to pay $453,733 in a settlement that accuses the department of maintaining an unconstitutional practice of prolonging stops to run warrant and i-card (investigation card) searches, "turning each stop into an unrelated fishing expedition and "subjecting our clients to harassment by police," Molly Griffard, staff attorney with the Cop Accountability reports.

NYPD agrees to prohibit officers from detaining anyone while running background checks on outstanding warrants, including in the event a person encounters police for minor violations, according to the class action lawsuit.

"This settlement marks a change in the NYPD's official policy and holds the NYPD accountable for infringing on the rights of New Yorkers," Griffard stated while neglecting to declare it particularly protects those NY citizens who are violent felons.

18. (2023) "A bit of magic, wonder and joy brought to you by the talented tappers at Dorrance Dance, performing their playful interpretation of "The Nutcracker Suite." First Lady Dr. Jill Biden touts the (latest) desecration of the White House in the ghastly performance of a Christmas video by Dorrance Dance, a tap dance company founded by Michelle Dorrance and Josette Wiggan in 2011. Just when you don't think it can get any worse it does when the troupe's website reveals its support of defunding the police, abolishing prisons, and diminishing Israel's standing in the world. Additionally, a dedicated section on the studio's homepage focuses on "social justice" and "resistance" and lists ways that "white people can take action in response to white and state-sanctioned violence."

19. (2023) The Colorado Supreme Court declares former President Donald Trump ineligible for the White House under the U.S. Constitution's insurrection clause and removes him from the state's presidential primary ballot. The decision from a court whose justices were all appointed by Democratic governors marks the first time in history that Section 3 of the 14th Amendment has been used to disqualify a presidential candidate.

"We do not reach these conclusions lightly. We are mindful of the magnitude and weight of the questions now before us. We are likewise mindful of our solemn duty to apply the law, without fear or favor, and without being swayed by public reaction to the decisions that the law mandates we reach," the pitiful court wrote. The decision comes with Trump having never been charged or convicted of any criminal acts related to the Jan 6 protests.

Rather than telling the truth that they are aware their landmark decision defies the Constitution, is a horrific attack on democracy and nothing more than a cowardly ploy to judicially control a presidential election by eliminating the most popular (and beloved) candidate in the field, the CO justices make no further statements and seemingly go into hiding.

20. (2023) Trump didn't mention the decision during a rally Tuesday evening in Waterloo, Iowa, but his campaign sent out a fundraising email citing what it called a "tyrannical ruling."

"I'm saying to New Yorkers, "You're angry and I'm angry, and the source of our discontent lies in DC." And we need to mobilize and rally and go to D.C. and say to the national government, "This is not fair what's happening to New York City!"

NY Mayor Eric Adams tells New Yorkers they must mobilize against President Joe Biden if they want to stop the budget cuts caused by his flood of destitute migrants into the Big Apple.

During a press conference this week, NYC Mayor Eric Adams calls on residents of The Big Apple to "mobilize" against the federal government over the migrant crisis. Despite being a "sanctuary city" for aliens, the Dem mayor has complained frequently that the city cannot cope with the tens of thousands of migrants pouring into the city. Adams previously announced a staggering $7 billion in cuts to the city's budget to house, clothe, and feed illegal aliens. He and other Dems were largely silent when these migrants were overrunning red states like Texas.

Adams has not received the billions of dollars in aid he expected from the Biden administration. Now, it appears he wants New Yorkers to travel to D.C. and protest over what is going on.

The mayor's poll numbers have been devastated by the migrant crisis, as voters blame him for migrants camping out in hotels, parks, and public spaces.

21. (2023) White House Bureau Chief for Politico Jonathan Lemire writes that" Hunter Biden is acutely aware of his situation and that in recent conversations with family and friends, he has worried that he might have to flee the country if Donald Trump is elected president again."

22. (2023) The Post Millennial reports that a new study from the British journal PLOS One suggests that human beings may be a cause of global warming, not just in our actions, but by breathing. The idea is that people breathe out "small, elevated concentrations of methane (CH_4) and nitrous oxide (N_2O), both of which contribute to global warming."

The new report from climate alarmists in the UK accuses human beings of contributing to 0.1 percent of "greenhouse gas," just by breathing. The study states "that humans are fueling global warming by just exhaling from lungs." With so many Americans already fed up with climate alarmists who advocate banning meat, gas stoves, plastic straws, and single-family housing, the new demands that they stop breathing may be the last (banned) straw!

23. (2023) A report by the Center for Immigration Studies reveals that 59 percent of households led by illegal immigrants use at least one major taxpayer-funded welfare program, far higher than the 39 percent of U.S.-born households.

Authored by CIS analysts Steven Camarota and Karen Zeigler, the study relied on newly released data from the 2022 Survey of Income and Program Participation (SIPP), shedding light on the burden carried by U.S. taxpayers by illegal immigration. Government-funded social programs typically are not offered to illegal aliens.

However, CIS reported that those with children born in the U.S. can bypass these restrictions by accessing benefits provided to their children. The Biden White House is reportedly unhappy with the number and vows they won't rest until 100% of illegal aliens are receiving welfare.

24. (2023) Finally, Joe Biden receives some good news as he officially picks up a 2024 endorsement from "The Order of Nine Angels," a Satanic cult founded in the UK in the 1970s. "The Order" states on its website that

"democracy is failing; worldwide nations are going broke, preparing for war, inundated with refugees, beset by internal refugees, ruled by careerist psychopaths, and perhaps most ominously, electing leaders who are associated with foreign powers. We want to rush into the abyss so that the end of history can come to its natural terminus and a new Dark Age will be visited upon the Earth."

"In this new era," the endorsement continues, "might will make right, the claw and tooth will always be red, and blood will cross the land like an ever-flowing stream. The strong will oppress the weak, the weak will die, and natural selection will resume. This can only happen through weak humanist leadership that will stumble its way into war, famine, recession, terrorism, corruption, and human misery."

Ultimately, you have to give The Order of 9 credit for picking the right candidate to accomplish that job!

25. (2022) "In 2023, it's our hope that we'll all remember the wisdom of the seven principles of Kwanzaa, especially the values of unity and faith, as we work to make the promise of our nation real in the lives of every American."

In a pre-recorded video posted to Twitter, Joe and Dr. Jill Biden stand before a "kinara" to celebrate Kwanzaa. While acknowledging Kwanzaa is fine it is almost impossible to imagine two more insincere people making the gesture.

Enter VP Kamala Harris who chimes in with her own Kwanzaa childhood story. "I was the little girl who celebrated Kwanzaa. Growing up, Kwanzaa was always a special time, we came together with generations of friends and family and neighbors. There were never enough chairs, so my sister and I and the other children would often sit on the floor, and together we lit the candles of the kinara, and then the elders would talk about how Kwanzaa is a time to celebrate culture, community and family, and they of course taught us about the seven principles."

It should be noted Kamala grew up in Canada and is of Indian and Jamaican ancestry. Additionally, there doesn't appear to be a single photo documenting her celebrating the holiday with "the elders" and her other extended family while celebrating Kwanzaa in Montreal.

26. (2023) California stores with more than 500 employees will soon be fined for not having a "gender-neutral" toy section once a new state law kicks in Jan. 1. The bill, signed in 2021 by Gavin Newsom, will force stores that sell childcare items or toys to pay a $500 fine should the store fail to create a gender-neutral toy section for kids 12 years old and under.

With soaring crime, inflation, home unaffordability, open borders, and Democrat politics already generating a mass exodus of Californians from the state, Newsom nails the source of Cali's problems: that toy stores have failed to create "gender-neutral toys" for children. Can you hear FL Governor Ron DeSantis guffawing in the background?

27. (2021) "I mean, that's crazy. The guy should be fired on the spot!" Dr. Anthony Fauci declares Fox News host Jesse Watters should be fired for using "violent language" at a conservative conference to encourage attendees to conduct an ambush interview with him in hopes of creating a viral

moment. Watters made his remarks Monday at the right-wing Turning Points USA conference where he gave students a playbook on how to record a viral moment that Fox News would air and that other right-wing outlets would amplify. "Now you go in for the kill shot. The kill shot? With an ambush? Deadly. Because he doesn't see it coming," Watters told his audience.

Fauci reacted with shock to Watters' "awful" comments while also acknowledging that it's "very likely" Watters would be held "unaccountable" by Fox News.

Dr. Fauci finally gets something right as Fox does indeed defend Watters stating, "Based on watching the full clip and reading the entire transcript, it's more than clear that Jesse Watters was using a metaphor for asking hard-hitting questions to Dr. Fauci about gain-of-function research and his words have been twisted completely out of context."

"The only thing that I have ever done throughout these two years is to encourage people to practice good public health practices: to get vaccinated, to be careful in public settings, to wear a mask. And for that you have some guy out there saying that people should be giving me a kill shot to ambush me? I mean, what kind of craziness is there in society these days?" Fauci lamented.

It is hard to refute the doctor's comment regarding societal "craziness" during the last two years. It's almost as if some crazed, lunatic fraud has been ordering Americans to obey his orders to completely shut down their lives until said "crazed, lunatic fraud" gives his okay to resume them.

28. (2021) Joe Biden asks the Supreme Court for permission to end the Trump-era "remain in Mexico" policy, which requires non-Mexican migrants to stay in Mexico until their US immigration court dates.

In August, a federal judge in Texas ordered the revival of the policy after DHS attempted to end the program. An appeals court also ruled against the administration, which began re-implementing the program earlier in the month.

When the federal appeals court blocked President Joe Biden's attempt to end the immigration program, it said the administration's efforts did not comply with the Administrative Procedure Act, which sets out specific processes that agencies must go through in unveiling new policies.

The court also said the effort violated an immigration law that says noncitizens "shall" be detained or returned to the countries from where they arrived while their immigration proceedings move forward.

While there is no way to confirm this, anonymous sources say Biden was infuriated by the court's decision and screamed, "How in the hell am I supposed to destroy America with all this red tape? I'm telling you, it's malarkey, man!"

29. (2020) "We're pleased to have taken it down this morning." A spokeswoman for Boston Mayor Marty Walsh reports the good news that the "Emancipation Group" statue, which portrays President Lincoln in a suit standing above a partially dressed former slave rising from broken shackles and has stood in Park Square since 1879 "has been removed and relocated to a storage facility."

30. (2021) "These events are intended as an observance of reflection, remembrance and recommitment, in a spirit of unity, patriotism and prayerfulness." "Prayerful" Nancy Pelosi announces to her Dem colleagues that "a slate of events" around the US Capitol is being scheduled to commemorate the one-year anniversary of the January 6 "insurrection" and will feature a "Historic Perspective" conversation between historians Doris Kearns Goodwin and Jon Meacham "to establish and preserve the narrative of January 6th!"

While Pelosi & Friends are indeed dedicated to preserving the Jan 6 "narrative" they are unequivocally opposed to preserving the "TRUTH!"
31. (2019) "If he'd take it, yes." Dem presidential candidate and former VP Joe Biden says that, if elected, he would nominate former President Barack Obama to the to the Supreme Court - if Obama would accept it.

Judging by the level of integrity Biden demands of his appointees one can't help but wonder if a nomination of Hunter to the high court isn't in the works.

Postlude

"History doesn't repeat itself, but it often rhymes."
Mark Twain, *The Adventures of Tom Sawyer*

As we bid farewell to the failures, fiascos, and fumbling missteps of the Democratic party that have been recounted in this volume, let us not be swayed by the temptation to consign them to the annals of forgotten history and leave future rhymes unrecognized.

While the passage of time may dim our recollection of the most recent current events already fading from memory, the echoes of these stories must resonate through the corridors of our collective memory, serving as guideposts for the journey ahead.

In an era where the clamor of the current media trend often drowns out the whispers of the most recent conflagration, it is imperative that we pause to reflect and heed the wisdom of those who have come before us. They have spent countless hours laying pen to paper, finger to typewriter, voice to transcription in an effort to keep the memory of the past alive in the future.

For in chronicled narratives lie hard-won lessons of perseverance, courage, and resilience—lessons that can and will illuminate the path toward a more patriotic and enlightened society, upholding our Constitution and our rights as citizens of the great country of the United States of America.

Though the road may be fraught with obstacles from the Left (and unfortunately also the Right), we must march forward undeterred, fueled by the knowledge that our actions today to remember what has been will shape the world of tomorrow, and hopefully avoid a repeat.

Let us embrace the responsibility entrusted to us, to safeguard these stories not only for our own edification, but also for the enlightenment of generations yet to come.

So, as we turn the final page, let us pledge to preserve the memory and the cause-and-effect of the actions of the Democratic party in recent times.

For it is in remembering that we must record history in order to study and learn from it, and in doing so, lay the foundations for a better, brighter tomorrow for our children and our grandchildren.

To this purpose was this content compiled and produced.

–Brandon Vallorani
Tolle Lege Press

www.ingramcontent.com/pod-product-compliance
Lightning Source LLC
Chambersburg PA
CBHW032055150426
43194CB00006B/532